My Sacred Bull - 2

Insights from

Reason and Religion

In Arrangement with *Financial Chronicle*

My Sacred Bull - 2

Insights from
Reason and Religion
In Arrangement with *Financial Chronicle*

Kuruvilla Pandikattu SJ
Professor of Physics, Philosophy and Religion
Jnana-Deepa Vidyapeeth, Pune

CWI
Christian World Imprints™

First Published in 2015 by

Christian World Imprints™
Christian Publishing & Books from India
H-12 Bali Nagar, **New Delhi-110015**
info@christianworldimprints.com
www.ChristianWorldImprints.com
Phone: +91 11 25465925

ISBN-13: 978-93-5148-070-9 ISBN-10: 93-5148-070-4

Cataloging in Publication Data--DK

Courtesy: D.K. Agencies (P) Ltd. <docinfo@dkagencies.com>

Pandikattu, Kuruvila, author.

Insights from reason and religion : in arrangement with Financial chronicle / Kuruvilla Pandikattu SJ.

pages cm. -- (My sacred bull ; 2)

Includes bibliographical references (pages) and index.

ISBN 9789351480709

ISBN 9351480704

1. Religion and science. 2. Science and spiritualism. I. Title. II. Series: My sacred bull ; 2.

DDC 201.65 23

Printed at Replika Press Pvt. Ltd.

Dedicated to:

The students and staff – academic and domestic – who have contributed to the growth of Jnana-Deepa Vidyapeeth and Papal Seminary (founded at Kandy in 1983) during the last sixty (1955-2015) years in Pune.

The Book

Today more and more people are getting convinced that the future humanity depends on how science and religion can collaborate with each other. This book contains short articles on reason (science) and religion (spirituality) meant for a general audience, who may or may not be organisationally religious. They are meant to inspire a band of young and old women and men to think deeply about themselves, leading to deeper insights and wisdom. It is the author's conviction that genuine spirituality is open-ended and reaches to the other in love and compassion.

Open-minded and visionary, these articles are meant to touch the daily life of busy people who are fully involved in the struggle and success of daily life. So, the articles are limited to 625 words. They attempt to enhance the precious and vulnerable life by reaching out to others. It assumes that only when we can maintain the healthy tension between the spiritual and material aspects of life, we become more authentic.

The Author has roughly categorized the articles into the following nine sections:

- Human Uniqueness
- Human Compassion
- Mind and Body
- Science and Religion
- Truth and Reality
- Towards Greater Authenticity
- Evolving Spirituality
- Openness to the Deeper
- Lessons from Life

These articles appeared in the "My Mind" Op-Ed Column of *Financial Chronicle* (www.mydigitalfc.com).

The Author

Dr. Kuruvilla Pandikattu (born 1957-) is Professor of Physics, Philosophy and Religion at Jnana-Deepa Vidyapeeth, Pune, India, since 1996. He has three Masters' Degrees in Physics and Philosophy and two Doctorates in Philosophy and Theology to his credit. He has been actively involved in dialogue between science and religion. Author of more than 30 books and 160 academic articles, Pandikattu is a Jesuit priest belonging to Dumka-Raiganj Province, India. He has been involved in organising more than 20 national and international conferences on science-religion dialogue. He has visited more than 15 countries and attended more than 100 conferences on Philosophy, Theology and Science-Religion Dialogue. Because of his creative and committed writings, he has been in the editorial board of five philosophical/religious journals. He is a renowned author, spiritual leader, motivational speaker and research guide. His main topics of research are: Anthropology, Eschatology and Transhumanism. He may be contacted at kuru@kuru.in (personal) or kuru@jdv.edu.in (professional). Site: www.kuru.in

Foreword

Six years ago, *Financial Chronicle* (FC), India's first global business networking platform, was looking for spiritually focused, knowledge-driven content to inspire and enrich its educated audience of business leaders, managers and corporate executives. Editor-in-chief Shubhrangshu Roy, who conceived the daily newspaper and initiated the project "My Sacred Bull," on the editorial page of Financial Chronicle, asked me to discover an enlightened thinker to address the existential yearnings of intelligent India and FC's wider global audience.

I turned to Professor Kuruvilla Pandikattu SJ for his innate wisdom. He is a priest, physicist and philosopher, adorned with three masters' degrees and two doctorates. His creative spirit and open vision had long inspired me. The professor-priest readily obliged, taking pen to paper week after week to script a volume that has now acquired epic proportions. His path breaking column is deeply relished and respected by FC's global band of dedicated readers.

Prof Pandikattu's articles stand out for three characteristics that are uncommon in both spiritual and scientific discourses:

1. *Contextual sensitivity:* Normally he takes up a current event – from politics, science or religion – and reflects on it giving it a spiritual basis and contemporary relevance.
2. *Religious openness:* Committed to his Catholic faith, his critical and creative acceptance of other religious and non-religious traditions is extraordinary. Without falling into eclecticism, he has a way of drawing the positive aspect of every event.
3. *Forward movement:* His writings pursue our quest as individuals and communities, to move ahead in our

> pilgrimage of life, conquering new peaks. He is convinced of the Spirit working within us to move us to another level, where human beings can live in peace and harmony, affirming and respecting the differences that exist among each other.

By and large, these spiritual essays are non-denominational and are not limited to any religious group. At the same time, they open the inquisitive spirit in us and thus widen our experience. As such, his columns are very inspiring and forward-looking.

I am happy to note that he has handpicked the best of the first hundred articles that he has scripted for FC and is publishing them in this book: "My Sacred Bull: Insights from Reason and Religion in Arrangement with *Financial Chronicle.*" As of today more than 250 well-appreciated articles of Prof Pandikattu have appeared in our "My Sacred Bull" column, which has been appearing in the "My Mind" section of *Financial Chronicle* for six years now. Truly a great achievement! I recommend this book whole-heartedly for its inquisitiveness, spiritual depth and universal openness.

Dr. Michael Gonsalves
Senior Assistant Editor
Financial Chronicle

Acknowledgements

In bringing out this book, I am immensely grateful to Mr. Shubhrangshu Roy, the Chief Operating Editor and Editor-in-chief, *Financial Chronicle*, who has requested me to write these articles.

I am also indebted to Dr Michael Gonsalves, Senior Assistant Editor, *Financial Chronicle*, who has been constantly urging me to contribute my share to it.

With a deep sense of gratitude, I want to acknowledge the role played by the staff and students of Papal Seminary, Pune and Jnana-Deepa Vidyapeeth, Pune, India, for providing me with the facilities and opportunities for these insights. I am particularly grateful to Rev. Fr. Arun Kumar SJ for his meticulous editorial contribution.

Finally, I am indeed grateful to the Almighty, who makes all things possible, so that we may "live, move and have our being" in Him, who is our Everything.

Kuruvilla Pandikattu SJ

Contents

Mind and Body

Science and Religion

Truth and Reality

Towards Greater Authenticity

Evolving Spirituality

Openness to the Deeper

Lessons from Life

Introduction

How do we find meaning in life? How do we cope with our existence? In order to answer these questions from scientific and religious perspectives, I have been writing few articles.

The articles in this book are especially written for *Financial Chronicle* (FC), which is the Hyderabad-based Deccan Chronicle Holdings Ltd, that was launched on 16 April, 2008, by India's youngest team of media professionals, and in the shortest-ever run-up for a newspaper.

As such the articles are meant for general audience, who may or may not be organisationally religious. They are meant to inspire a band of young men and women to think deeply about themselves, leading to deeper insights and wisdom.

Open-minded and thought-provoking, these articles are meant to touch the daily life of busy people who are fully involved in the struggle and success of daily life. So, each article is limited to 625 words. These articles attempt to provide them with both roots and wings: roots that will give them a sense of belonging to the world and wings that will take us beyond to unlimited possibilities.

For better clarity and convenience, these articles are divided into nine approximate and arbitrary sections.

I. Human Uniqueness
II. Human Compassion
III. Mind and Body
IV. Science and Religion
V. Truth and Reality
VI. Towards Greater Authenticity
VII. Evolving Spirituality
VIII. Openness to the Deeper
IX. Lessons from Life

In writing these articles, I presume that day to day events can be source of spiritual depth. That every seeking – religious, scientific, affective or rational – leads to the depth which invites us to lead lives that are more authentic and genuine. That we can find fulfilment in life only in and through our neighbours. That the fullness of life – at least the traces of it – can be experienced here and now.

So, it is my fervent hope that these articles, which may be disconnected in themselves, will lead some of us to a deeper sense of reality and a profound sense of wonder – at ourselves, at the larger world outside and inside. May we experience the profound religiosity in everyday things and events of life!

Human Uniqueness

1

We Need to be Open to the Whole of Life

The ability to identify the self and the non-self enable cells in more sophisticated animals to ward off invading infections, but it is critical to even simpler organisms such as social amoebae. The amoeba exists as a single cell when times are good. But, when there is not enough food, the cells aggregate and become multi-cellular fruiting bodies with a dead stalk and live spores, enabling the cells to survive and pass on genes. When the social amoeba aggregates, it prefers to do so with "kin", the cells that are genetically similar to it, *Science Daily* reported in June (Baylor College of Medicine 2011).

Researchers at Baylor College of Medicine, Texas, have identified the genetic "lock and key" that enable the amoeba to tell kin from non-kin. "We hypothesised that the molecules that enable these cells to tell kin from non-kin would have properties similar to those of membrane-spanning proteins that contain immunoglobulin folds," said Gad Shaulsky, professor of molecular and human genetics and one of the authors of this report.

Just as the uniforms of armies enable the soldier to differentiate friend from foe, these amoebae use the protruding proteins as a kind of flag. In this case, the flag that protruded differs among strains of the amoeba. These differences are critical to the kin/non-kin discrimination.

They identified "suspect proteins" called TgrB1 and TgrC1. "Our hypothesis was that TgrB1 on the membrane of one cell recognises TgrC1 on the membrane of another," said Shaulsky. "The two cells stick together, and the proteins act like a lock and key. If your key matches my lock, you stay and we develop together. If your key does not match my lock, you cannot participate" (Baylor College of Medicine 2011).

In a complicated series of experiments, they removed the "suspect proteins" together or one by one. The result was the same. If the "suspect protein" on one cell came from the same strain as that on the other, the cells could cooperate. If either one of the proteins or both were from foreign strains, they could not aggregate with cells that had proteins from the original strain.

> Differences may be enabling but we need to acknowledge that differences are rooted in our commonality.

No matter how they modified "suspect proteins" in the amoeba, those proteins remained the key to determining kin/non-kin. "It's as though you had a blue lock and a blue key and a yellow lock and a yellow key," claimed Shaulsky. "If one cell has the blue lock and the other the blue key, then they can cooperate. They see each other as kin. However, if one cell has a blue key and the other a yellow lock, it will not work."

To determine if the cells are actually adhering to one another, they marked one population green and the other red. They separated them into single cells and then incubated the cells together. The cells that had the same "suspect proteins" stuck together into red-green aggregates. "As long as they have a shared lock and key set, then they can aggregate," said Shaulsky. "This is the first demonstration in a unicellular organism that immunoglobulin-like molecules are participating in self/non-self discrimination."

This research enables us to see how our idea of the self has evolved right from the beginning of life. Though highly complex, humans still retain a similar set of capabilities that enable us to differentiate ourselves from others. In addition, we can distinguish our kith and kin from others.

Differences may be enabling but we need to acknowledge that differences are rooted in our commonality. Although, we may favour our kith and kin, we need to be open to the whole of life. Truly, we are related to every form of life and non-life!

2

Drawing on Our Inner Resilience

Recently, while sharing with a spiritual person my underlying fear and anxieties that I simply can't handle, he listened to me with empathy and compassion. After a moment of pause, he looked into my eyes and said, "It's important to realise that you have resources to handle even more challenges."

As I took a step back and allowed what he said to resonate within me, I was touched. First of all, I appreciated his acknowledgment and reminder. Secondly, it allowed me to take inventory of some of the adversity I've overcome in my life. Thirdly, it convinced me of my resilience, which is a spiritual resource. And, finally, after my conversation with the spiritual master, I realised more and more about the power of the human spirit.

> We can create an even deeper and more authentic sense of self confidence.

In just about every situation and circumstance in life, we really do have more resource than is required to not only 'deal' with what's happening, but to thrive in the face of such adversities. As the saying goes, 'if it doesn't kill you, it makes you stronger'. I don't believe that we have to necessarily suffer and struggle in order to grow and evolve in life. Still, one of the best things we can do when dealing with challenges is 'to look for the gifts and find the gold in the situation' as much as possible.

Confronted with a challenging situation, we can visualise how it plays out in our life and how it has played out in our past. Often, we have things happen that initially we don't think we can handle– sometimes these are things we consider 'bad' and sometimes they're things we consider to be 'good.'

However, as we look back over the course of our lives, we can probably find very many instances, when we were able to overcome challenges, deal with fear, rise above limiting beliefs, and deal with things we thought we could never manage. In this context, it is true that 'circumstances don't define you, they reveal you'. Thus, fostering resilience and dwelling on our spiritual resources is one of the best means of using our adversities for our growth.

To foster resilience, it is good to recall to mind all that we have already achieved, experienced and overcome. We can make the inventory of our life from the perspective of resilience. We can think about all the times we have dealt with change, loss, newness, fear, pain, disappointment and failure – and have been able to work through it.

We have, probably, also had many experiences in life where wonderful things and exciting opportunities showed up and we were able to step up and take the experience of life to a whole new level. Even though we are all unique, our stories are different, and we have varying personalities and life experiences, most of us have achieved, experienced, and overcome a lot in our lives up to this point. By remembering this and acknowledging ourselves for it, "we can create an even deeper and more authentic sense of self confidence," as the motivational speaker Mike Robbins asserts (Robbins 2011).

Regardless of what we are struggling with right now–however hard, easy, challenging, or wonderful things are–we truly have more than is required by any of the challenges in our lives. And, the more we remember this and live from this perspective, the more freedom, power, and peace of mind we'll experience. For a believer, such a resilience and spiritual depth emerges from his encounter with the Divine. As spiritual persons, we can draw on the power of human resilience, turning challenges into opportunities for our growth.

3

Fulfilling Our Life's Purpose

Saadi, 12th century Persian poet, wrote, "Every being is intended to be on earth for a certain purpose" (Cited in Loma, House & Magazine 2012). If so, "Why can't I find the purpose of my life?" Many people, sometimes in their lives, feel that they don't know what they're really here, for, on this planet. They long for that 'certain something' that defines and integrates their lives.

Many turn to the books and programmes that purport to identify their life's purpose, but most come away dissatisfied. And yet, many do find and live in harmony with their life's purpose. First, I think everyone feels a pull towards some defining purpose in his or her life, no matter how much it may have become shrouded along the way. In fact, all forms of life, all natural phenomena, have some purpose. There's always movement or evolution towards some kind of outcome or fulfillment – whether it's a tree that produces fruit, or clouds that form to produce rain. But we, humans, become so enraptured by our daily activities, engagements, goals and so on, that our awareness of the unique life purpose is easily dimmed, according to business psychologist and psychotherapist, Douglas LaBier in *The Huffington Post* (LaBier 2011).

> The larger purpose of life puts in context so many of our little worries!

And there are consequences to not knowing or finding your purpose. In fact, there are men and women who've become successful in their work and relationships – their outer lives – and yet they feel hollow, unfulfilled. They describe their feeling of being 'off-track' in some way, despite a conventionally successful life. Sometimes they wonder if they've been on the 'wrong' path all along – chosen the wrong career, or set on the wrong goal. Or perhaps they haven't realised that their chosen path could be more meaningful or purposeful to them.

One thing is clear, that the consequences of not finding their purpose include chronic, lingering dissatisfaction: an absence of inner peace and a sense of not being fully in sync with your inner self. That's because their true inner self knows that the purpose of their life is out of sync with their outer life. The latter is often a false self, but they have identified themselves with it because it has been so rewarding to their ego.

Most people retain at least a glimmer of awareness of their life's purpose within their inner being. It often feels like a leaning or an inclination, which continues to pull you. Sometimes it is right in front of your eyes but you don't allow yourself to see it, like when you're hunting for your missing keys and then discover that they've been right in front of you the whole time. For example, Douglas LaBier describes an investment adviser, who found himself doing more and more work with charity organisations (LaBier 2011). He finally realized that what he felt most in sync with was hands-on work helping people. That was the part he enjoyed about his work, not the money managing per se. Helping people was his true calling, and it was staring at him in the face, the whole time.

Those who experience a clear inclination but don't pursue or fulfill it remain incomplete and dissatisfied. When we are living in accordance with our life's purpose, we view all of the above as part of what we encounter along the road. They don't distract us from that larger vision, our ideal, which is like a magnet steadily pulling us towards it.

On the other hand, the larger goal gives us new impetus to our concrete desires and particular aims. Our life becomes much more coherent and focused, even when it is challenging. For, the larger purpose of life puts in context so many of our little worries!

4

A Life of Simplicity Amid the City Bling

Most spiritual leaders agree that simplicity is a virtue in itself. Therefore, it is important to recognise inaccurate stereotypes about the simple life because they make it seem impractical and ill-suited for our contemporary life-style. As Duane Elgin, the author of *Voluntary Simplicity* holds, "it is because of certain misconceptions that equate simplicity with abject poverty, returning to the village life and living without beauty."

Simplicity does not mean poverty. Although some spiritual traditions have advocated a life of extreme renunciation, it is misleading to equate simplicity with poverty. Poverty is involuntary and debilitating; whereas simplicity is voluntary and enabling. A life of conscious simplicity can have both a beauty and a functional integrity that elevates the human spirit. Poverty fosters a sense of helplessness, passivity and despair, whereas voluntary simplicity fosters a sense of personal empowerment and creative engagement. Historically, those choosing a simpler life have sought the golden mean – an aesthetic balance between poverty and excess. Instead of placing primary emphasis on material riches, they sought to develop experiential riches. Certainly, simplicity is not misery, which they try to eliminate.

Simplicity does not mean rural life. In the popular imagination there is a tendency to equate the simple life with that of the American poet and idealist Henry David Thoreau, who also influenced the Father of Our Nation. It is assumed that to be simple, people must live in an isolated and rural environment. Interestingly, Thoreau was not a hermit during his stay at the cabin in the woods. In fact, his famous cabin was roughly a mile from town, and every day or two he would walk into town. His cabin was so close to a nearby highway that he could "smell the pipe smoke of passing travelers." Thoreau wrote that he had "more visitors while I lived in the woods than in any other period of my life" (Elgin 2011). The romanticised image of rural living does not fit modern reality, as a majority of people, choosing a life of simplicity, do not live in the backwoods or rural settings; they do not even need to. While green living brings with it a reverence for nature, it does not require moving to a rural setting. Instead of a 'back to the villages' movement, it is more accurate to describe simplicity as a 'make the most of wherever you are' movement. Increasingly, that means adapting creatively to a rapidly changing world, in the context of big cities and suburbs, with their busy lifestyle.

Simplicity liberates the aesthetic sense 'by freeing things from artificial encumbrances'.

Simplicity means living with beauty. The simple life is sometimes viewed as an approach to living that advocates a barren plainness and denies the value of beauty and aesthetics. While the puritans, for example, were suspicious of the arts, most advocates of simplicity have seen it as essential for revealing the natural beauty of things. Many who adopt a simpler life would agree with Pablo Picasso that "art is the elimination of the unnecessary." Similarly, Leonardo da Vinci said, "Simplicity is the ultimate sophistication." Frederic Chopin holds that, "Simplicity is the final achievement... the crowning reward of art."

Today, we are in need of an 'organic simplicity' that blends harmoniously with the natural environment, as Duane Elgin holds. In fact, simplicity liberates the aesthetic sense 'by freeing things from artificial encumbrances.' From a spiritual perspective, simplicity removes the 'obscuring clutter and discloses the life-energy that infuses all things.' Thus, simplicity brings with itself beauty and elegance that is essentially a part of the Divine. It is 'a way of life that is outwardly simple and inwardly rich' (Elgin 2011).

5

Technology Takes Control of Our Lives

In the beginning of the modern age, telegraphs and trains gave birth to the idea that convenience is more important than content and "speedier means" could make up for "unimproved ends". Philosopher Henry David Thoreau countered, "The man whose horse trots a mile in a minute does not carry the most important messages." Marshall McLuhan, a Canadian media scholar, warned, "When things come at you very fast, naturally, you lose touch with yourself." In the 1970s, Alvin Toffler, an American futurist, spoke of the "future shock" as a certain psychological state of individuals and entire societies dealing with "too much change in too short a period of time" (Toffler 1970). Thomas Merton, a Cistercian monk, urged us to get out of the rat race and said, "Man was made for the highest activity, which is, in fact, his rest."

Coming to contemporary times, it is estimated that an average American teenager deals with 75 text messages a day. One girl even managed to handle an average of 10,000 messages every 24 hours for one full month. In our computer world, multi-tasking has become essential and in the process of saving time, we end up having no time for ourselves. Although today's technology claims to make life more comfortable and facilitates the process of living, in fact, it tends to take control of us, slowly and surely. They force us to tune into "breaking news" that is happening almost daily. As Pico Iyer, the author of *The Man Within My Head* (Iyer 2012), writes in *The New York Times*, the traditional distinctions that used to guide and steady us – between Sunday and Monday, public and private, here and there – are also disappearing (Iyer 2011).

So, we have more to speak and less to say, maybe because we're too busy communicating. As Iyer reminds us "we're rushing to meet so many deadlines that we hardly register that what we need most are lifelines" (Iyer 2011). We need to slow down, without becoming less productive. We need to relax without wasting our life. We need to progress without being enslaved by it.

This is the dilemma we are in. "The central paradox of the machines that have made our lives so much brighter, quicker, longer and healthier is that they cannot teach us how to make the best use of them," Iyer (2011) says. All the data in the world cannot teach us how to prioritise; images don't show us how to process them. The danger is that all our life becomes samsara or a series of distractions. French philosopher Blaise Pascal put it tersely, "Distraction is the only thing that consoles us for our miseries; and yet, it is itself the greatest of our miseries." He added that human problems come from our inability to sit quietly in a room alone.

The only way we can deal with this dilemma is by drawing "the emotional and moral clarity" that comes from our inner strength and our spiritual resources. Such spiritual resources make us feel better – calmer, happier and more focused – with the particular work that we do. They enable us to stay connected, while at the same time, enable us to maintain some distance. It encourages us to be fully involved while retaining some aloofness for we can see the whole and understand it better, only when we are also away from it.

So, coping with our contemporary world demands that we perceive the essential, not always the new things. It demands being creatively alone. Here the distinction that German thinker, Paul Tillich, makes between loneliness and solitude is very apt. "Loneliness expresses the pain of being alone and solitude expresses the glory of being alone," Tillich said (cited in Iyer 2011).

Distraction is the only thing that consoles us for our miseries; and yet, it is itself the greatest of our miseries.

6

The Marvelous Machine Maker

Historically seen, the evolution of machine intelligence is marvelous. First they out-calculated us in simple math. Then they replaced us on the assembly lines, explored places we couldn't get to. Then in 1997, the chess playing machine Deep Blue won the match against world champion Garry Kasparov even beat our champions at chess. In February 2011, Watson, a gigantic computer created by IBM, beat the TV Show Quizz Program, "Jeopardy!" It is a marvelous feat that experts call "a technological breakthrough".

The next step for the programmers, as reported in *The Huffington Post*, is "to help doctors plow through blizzards of medical information. Watson could also help make Internet searches far more like a conversation than the hit-or-miss things they are now" (Borenstein & Jordan 2011).

Watson's victory raises the crucial question: What can we puny humans do that amazing machines cannot do or will never do? The answer, like all of "Jeopardy!," comes in the form of a question: Who – not what – dreamed up Watson? Who can truly marvel at the ingenuity of Watson? So far, only humans can.

"The way to think about this is: Can Watson decide to create Watson?" said Pradeep Khosla, of Carnegie Mellon University in Pittsburgh. Our ability to create and to marvel at it makes us unique. Some hold that along with the "spark of creation" what makes us unique are the pride we can take, the empathy we have with the winners and losers, and that magical mix of adrenaline and fear we experience.

Richard Doherty, a computer industry expert, thinks that IBM's advances with Watson are changing the way people think about artificial intelligence and how a computer can be programmed to give conversational answers – not merely lists of useless entries.

> What the computers really cannot do is to expose themselves to the marvelous and the mysterious.

However, some of Watson's creators say this breakthrough gives an extra appreciation for the more magnificent and mysterious machines, the humans. "I see human intelligence consuming machine intelligence, not the other way around," David Ferrucci, the IBM's lead researcher on Watson, said in an interview Wednesday. He added: "Humans are a different sort of intelligence. Our intelligence is so interconnected. The brain is so incredibly interconnected with itself, so interconnected with all the cells in our body, and has co-evolved with language and society and everything around it" (Borenstein & Jordan 2011).

He said further: "Humans are learning machines that live and experience the world and take in an enormous amount of information – what they see, what they taste, what they feel, and they're taking that in from the day they're born until the day they die." The ability of a machine to learn is the essence of the field of artificial intelligence.

But, what the computers really cannot do is to expose themselves to the marvelous and the mysterious. Humans can truly open themselves to the mysterious in the world. And the ability to create a marvelous machines adds to the marvel and mystery of themselves. Precisely at this point of wonder emerges philosophy and religion.

Thus, we can assert that as long as Watson and future computers cannot be made to make other machines and marvel at themselves, human can still claim uniqueness. But if one day the machines can really answer questions, solve problems, emphathise with others, wonder at themselves and discover the meaning of their existence, then they may be considered as equal to humans. Can such machines possess identity, freedom and dignity? We will have to wait a long time to answer that question.

But, already now we can humbly affirm. We humans do possess self-identity, freedom and dignity. So we can create things and wonder at ourselves. That is the mystery we live every day. There lies the greatness of the measly humans!

Human Compassion

7

Laughter can be a Remedy for Pain

Why do we feel good when we laugh? According to the latest scientific study, simple muscular exertions involved in producing the familiar ha, ha, ha, trigger an increase in endorphins, resulting in a feel-good effect. Since the beginning of humanity we have been trying to understand the deceptively simple and universal behaviour of human laughter. "Laughter is very weird stuff, actually," said Robin Dunbar, an evolutionary psychologist at Oxford. So, he took up this study, which indicates that laughter contributes to group bonding and may have been important in the evolution of highly social humans.

Social laughter, according to the result of the study, is "grooming at a distance." It fosters closeness in a group, the way one-on-one grooming or patting promote, and maintains bonds between individual primates of all sorts. In five sets of studies in the laboratory and one field study at comedy performances, Dunbar and colleagues tested resistance to pain both before and after bouts of social laughter. The findings eliminated the possibility that the pain resistance measured was the result of a general sense of well-being rather than actual laughter. It was actual, physical laughter that made them feel good. So they conclude: "The causal sequence is laughter triggers endorphin activation."

Robert R, Provine, a neuroscientist at the University of Maryland, Baltimore County, and author of *Laughter: A Scientific Investigation* (Provine 2000), opined that the study was "a significant contribution" to a field that dates back 2,000 years or so. He pointed out that the benefits of laughter have not been properly explored. Both Plato and Aristotle, Provine said, were concerned with the power of laughter to undermine authority. And he noted that the ancients were well aware that laughter could accompany raping and pillaging as well as "a comic tale told by the hearth." The present study was concerned with actual physical laughter that relaxes us. Dunbar was interested in relaxed, contagious social laughter, not the tyrant's cackle or the critique's cynical smile. To test the relationship of such physical laughter to pain resistance, Dunbar did a series of six experiments. In five, participants watched excerpts of comedy videos, neutral videos or videos meant to promote good feeling but not laughter.

Laughter is an early mechanism to bond social groups.

In the lab experiments, the participants were tested before and after seeing different combinations of videos. The results indicated that actual laughing increased pain resistance whereas simple good feeling in a group setting did not. Pain resistance, is used as an indicator of endorphin levels because their presence in the brain is difficult to test; the molecules would not appear in blood samples because they are among the brain chemicals that are prevented from entering circulating blood by the so-called blood brain barrier.

Further, Dunbar thinks laughter may have been favoured by evolution because it helped bring human groups together, the way other activities like dancing, singing and praying together do. Those activities also produce endorphins, he said, and physical activity is important in them as well. "Laughter is an early mechanism to bond social groups," he concluded. In fact, primates use it. Indeed, apes are known to laugh, although in a different way than humans. They pant. "Panting is the sound of rough-and-tumble play," Provine said. It becomes a "ritualisation" of the sound of play. And in the course of the evolution of human beings, he suggests, "Pant, pant becomes ha, ha." Similarly, in spiritual activities too, physical activities, including laughing and dancing together, have an important function. So we can afford to laugh it out!

8

Humor at the Workplace

People assume that kidding around at work isn't a good thing. But a research conducted by University of Missouri-Columbia shows that light humor affects the working environment positively.

Chris Robert, an expert and author in this field, said that "humor – particularly joking around about things associated with the job – actually has a positive impact in the workplace." Further, he concluded: "Occasional humor among colleagues, he said, enhances creativity, department cohesiveness and overall performance."

The conclusion was made after examining theories on humor and examining literature from a wide variety of disciplines that touch on the subject. They concluded that when it comes to business efficiency, "humor is serious business."

"Humor has a significant impact in organizations," said Robert, who is also a professor of psychology. "Humor isn't incompatible with goals of the workplace. It's not incompatible with the organization's desire to be competitive." Elaborating further, he argues that "humor is pretty important. It's not just clowning around and having fun; it has meaningful impact on cohesiveness in the workplace and communication quality among workers." He added: "The ability to appreciate humor, the ability to laugh and make other people

> Good humor is a tonic for mind and body. It is the best antidote for anxiety and depression. It is a business asset.

laugh actually has physiological effects on the body that cause people to become more bonded."

In their paper, Robert and Yan focus on three primary areas: (1) how humor works and its cognitive effects, which the researchers said influences creativity (2) why humor has a positive effect within an organization (3) the influence of humor on positive emotions and the link between positive emotions and improved performance in organizations, and how culture influences the use of humor – particularly in multinational companies where people might have differences in their sensibilities and sense of humor.

As reported in *Science Daily*, the author also noted that the context is very crucial to appreciating humour and so in his research, he paid special attention to "economic powerhouses such as China and India." He acknowledges that it is difficult to use humour in cross cultural situations. So he holds: "It's hard to know what's going to be funny or when to use humor. Some people have suggested that you just avoid it all together; don't be funny, don't try to make jokes. We basically reject that and offer some ground rules for understanding when and what kind of humor might be appropriate."

At the same time, it may be noted too much of fooling around may be unproductive, just as too much of seriousness. "Good humor is a tonic for mind and body. It is the best antidote for anxiety and depression. It is a business asset" (Greenville Kleisser). What Oscar Wild holds is applicable also of religion: "It is a curious fact that people are never so trivial as when they take themselves seriously." To find that right, healthy mixture is the key to a healthy environment and better efficiency.

The same is applicable to our spiritual relationship with God. Obviously when we take religion and religious principles too seriously, we tend to absolutise it and make it an idol. A little bit of fun, pun and humour in our spiritual life can bring about a liberative dimension in our spiritual growth.

For the really wise person can pray and play. Even when she is serious, she can also be little cynical. A bit of healthy, critical mistrust is essential for nurturing a relationship. Such a spiritual person can ask from God, implore and even joke with him. She can even scold

God and get annoyed with him. If we curtail that ability to see the funny side even of the most sacred spheres, we become less of humans.

9

The Humble and Helpful are Happy

We know that some personality types are more generous than others. A recent scientific study, reported in LiveScience, suggests that humble people are more willing to lend a helping hand than their arrogant counterparts (Bryner 2012).

The study showed that humble people "may be more down-to-earth than arrogant people, but, that doesn't mean they think poorly of themselves". The lead researcher Jordan LaBouff, of the University of Maine, elaborated: "In fact, rather than being insecure or reserved, humble people seem to be characterised by an accurate view of themselves, understanding of their strengths and weaknesses and are comfort[able] with them."

> Humble people may have more time, resources and attention to direct towards peers in need.

The study, published in *The Journal of Positive Psychology*, emphasises the positive side of humility. It is generally assumed that humble people make more effective and better-liked leaders than those who wear their achievements on their sleeve. Even so, very few studies have shown any effect of personality on helpfulness, said LaBouff, a psychologist. "The only other personality trait that has shown any effect (on helpful behaviour) is agreeableness, but, we found that humility predicted helping over and above that," LaBouff said (cited in Bryner 2012).

In the first of three studies, 117 participants indicated their level of humbleness and helpfulness. They also completed a questionnaire on the 'Big Five' personality traits, which are five basic attributes that describe the spectrum of human personality. Some scholarly works refer to the Big Five as the 'Five-Factor Model'. The model comprises five personality dimensions: Openness to experience, Conscientiousness, Extraversion, Agreeableness and Neuroticism (OCEAN). Each dimension consists of a number of more specific traits. For example, Extraversion includes related qualities like sociability, excitement-seeking and positive emotions.

Those in the study who indicated they were humble also tended to say they were helpful. The results were true even when the researchers accounted for personality factors, such as agreeableness, which could impact helpfulness. In order to make sure these results were accurate and that volunteers weren't either exaggerating or underreporting their humbleness, the team ran other studies using an implicit measure of humility.

For instance, in another related but different study, 90 students listened to a recording about an injured student who couldn't always make it to classes, which they were told might be broadcast later on the campus radio station. Each participant then indicated how many hours over the next three weeks they would be willing to meet with the injured student to help her out. Those who scored higher on humility offered more helping time than other students.

In another study, 103 participants completed both implicit and self-report measures of humility. For instance, students had to associate as quickly as possible traits that applied to themselves: Humble, modest, tolerant, down-to-earth, respectful and open-minded. Words co-related with its opposite were arrogance, immodest, egotistical and conceited. Here too, the researchers found more humility was linked to more helpfulness.

"One aspect of humility is relatively low self-focus; humble people may have more time, resources and attention to direct towards peers in need," said LaBouff (cited in Bryner 2012).We can, thus, assert that humble people tend to be more helpful and open, thus, making them more pro-social and happy.

10

Simplicity is True Sophistication

"Life is really simple, but we insist on making it complicated." This insight of Confucius has been widely accepted by spiritual geniuses of all times. In fact, as the alternative-economist E. F. Schumacher would claim, "Any intelligent fool can make things bigger, more complex, and more violent. It takes a touch of genius – and a lot of courage – to move in the opposite direction."

Simplicity implies giving up the clutter and distractions of our life. It implies giving up things we do not need. It also implies giving up mental, intellectual and spiritual clutter, which is in fact more demanding to give up. In fact, simplicity is not merely a lifestyle. It is a way of being, in truth the only viable way of life in our contemporary world. It has economic, political and spiritual dimensions. Further, it also indicates the very essence of our own selves and of the world. The American philosopher, Henry David Thoreau, was right when he claimed: "As you simplify your life, the laws of the universe will be simpler; solitude will not be solitude, poverty will not be poverty, nor weakness a weakness" (cited in Chang 2006: 652).

As you simplify your life, the laws of the universe will be simpler; solitude will not be solitude, poverty will not be poverty, nor weakness a weakness.

Thus, simplicity is affirming the spiritual depth and complexity of a person. Such simple, and not simplistic, persons can very well accept Einstein's axiom: "Everything should be made as simple as possible but not simpler." In our drive to understand the world we are tempted to over-simplify, to see less than what is there, and to fail to appreciate the complexity of what is there. We love to toss out the bits of the world that puzzle us; what remains is then so much more manageable.

Simplicity is the ultimate sophistication.

For practical purposes we need to make life manageable. But, to mistake our manageable world for the whole reality is a crime we commit against ourselves. There are many atheists who proclaim dogmatically that there just isn't any mystery worth thinking about in the world. At the same time, there are many believers who have ready-made answers for everything and they seem to know things better than God Himself.

It is obvious that life and reality have more layers than wh-at meets the eye. In navigating the complexity of the world, we need more than just information. We need wisdom. In The Tacit Dimension, the philosopher of science Michael Polanyi expressed this in the provocative phrase: "We can know more than we can tell." Our theories, equations, logical systems and theologies capture some of the truth of what they are describing, but they always fall short. In the gap between what is captured in our nets of understanding and the larger reality lies the mystery of the world – the things we know, in some way, but cannot tell.

Polanyi's insight indicates the genuinely constructive dialogue between religion and reality, between life and its complexities, which longs to be simple and elegant. Then we realise that simplicity can be beautiful, elegant and also captivating.

Thus simplicity, lived out transparently and innocently, leads to a depth: a depth that makes life meaningful in itself. Open to this depth, we easily realise that there is more to reality that we can ever imagine. Living in such simplicity, we can open ourselves to the incessant flow of life and we can resonate with its eternal and ever-changing dance. True to its innocence, we can trust everyone and still accept also the evil and wicked aspects of life, including our own life.

Thus, the call to genuineness and authenticity urges us to be simple and to realise its own limits. The world-renowned artist, Leonardo da Vinci, has put it succinctly: "Simplicity is the ultimate sophistication" (cited in Zbilut & Giuliani 2008: 1).

11

Shrinking Degrees of Separation

The idea of degrees of separation was introduced in the 1960s by the social psychologist Stanley Milgram. Milgram asked 296 volunteers to attempt to get a message to a random individual living in the Boston suburb of Sharon, Mass, USA. The volunteers were asked to send the message to a personal acquaintance who might better know the recipient's address (cited in Chan 2012: 68).

The problem that Milgram wanted to study was: How are human beings connected? Do we all belong to separate worlds, operating simultaneously but autonomously, so that the links between any two people, anywhere in the world, are few and distant? Or are we all bound up together in a grand, interlocking web?

Milgram explored his idea with a chain letter. He got the names of 160 people who lived in one part of United States and mailed each of them a packet. In the packet was the name and address of a stockbroker who worked in Boston. Each person was instructed to write his or her name on the packet and send it on to a friend or acquaintance whom he or she thought would get the packet closer to the stock-broker.

> Technology truly shrinks the world further, makes us more connected and brings us closer to each other.

In the end of the experiment it took an average of 5.2 people in the chain to get the letter to the stockholder – or six intermediary people. This introduced the notion of "six degrees of separation". That phrase is now so familiar that it is easy to lose sight of how surprising Milgram's findings were. Most of us don't have particularly broad and diverse groups of friends. Still in general we are connected to anyone else on the planet earth by six persons.

It must be emphasised that in the six degrees of separation, not all degrees are equal. Six degrees of separation doesn't mean that everyone is linked to everyone else in just six steps. It means that a very small number of people are linked to everyone else in a few steps, and the rest of us are linked to the world through those special few, as noted by the well known author, Malcolm Gladwell in his *Tipping Point* (Gladwell 2000).

Now the surprise! According to the Facebook data team released in November 2011, the number of degrees of separation between people appears to have shrunk – at least for the more than 721 million Facebook users. Recently, the researchers from the University of Milan analysed 721 million active Facebook users and their friend networks. This constitutes 10 per cent of the global population with 69 billion friendships among them. They found that 92 per cent of people are linked by four intermediate friends and 99.6 per cent of the users are within five friends apart.

Just to illustrate this: If, in Facebook, you have an average of 100 friends, that means you already have 10,000 friends of friends. If you include their 100 friends each, you're at 1 million people within three degrees of separation. At five degrees of separation you have 10 billion people linked to you, which is greater than the Earth's population, as Matt Parker notes in *The Guardian.*

The company's data team says that as Facebook has grown over the years, the global population on Facebook has steadily become more connected. The average distance between two random people on Facebook in 2008 was 5.28 connections. In November 2011, it was 4.74.

Thus, technology truly shrinks the world further, makes us more connected and brings us closer to each other. That, in itself, is positive! But the challenge for us at the spiritual realm is more drastic: Can we truly accept our own uniqueness and identity and at the same time allow the separation to vanish? At the spiritual level, we are all connected at a zero level of separation!

12

Recognising Faces in a Holistic Way

How do we recognise faces? Why do some people never forget a face? How do we retain the face of someone we have only causally met? Some better than others? What is the significance of recognising the face? A recent scientific study throws light on this phenomenon of recognising human faces. "Face recognition is an important social skill, but not all of us are equally good at it," says Beijing Normal University cognitive psychologist Jia Liu. A recent study by Liu and colleagues provides the first experimental evidence that the inequality of abilities is rooted in the unique way in which the mind perceives faces. "Individuals who process faces more holistically"– that is, as an integrated whole –"are better at face recognition," says Liu. In daily life, we recognise faces both holistically and the opposite, "analytically". Analytic recognition is picking out individual parts, such as eyes or nose. But, while the brain uses analytical processing for different kinds of recognition – like that of a car, toy or animals –"holistic processing is thought to be especially critical to face recognition," says Liu (cited in Association for Psychological Science 2011).

> Spiritual openness is the ability to perceive reality in an integrated, comprehensive and a deeper way.

The researchers first measured the ability of study participants – 337 male and female students – to remember whole faces. They used tasks in which they had to select studied faces from among unfamiliar ones. The holistic processing of the face was done through composite-face effect (CFE) and whole-part effect (WPE), as reported in December 2011 issue of *Science Daily*. The composite-face effect (CFE) shows up when two faces are split horizontally and stuck together. The researchers found that it is easier to identify the top half-face when it's misaligned with the bottom one than when the two halves are fitted smoothly together. "That's because our brain automatically combines them to form a new"– and unfamiliar –"face," says Liu. This indicates holistic processing. In whole-part effect (WPE) people are shown a face, then asked to recognise a part of it – say, the nose. They do better when the feature is presented within the whole face than when it stands on its own among other noses: again, we can better recognise the nose that is integrated into the whole face.

The results, published in *Psychological Science,* a journal published by the Association for Psychological Science, are noteworthy: Participants who scored higher on CFE and WPE – that is, who did well in holistic processing – also performed better at the first task of recognising faces. It was also found that there was no link between facial recognition and general intelligence, suggesting that face processing is unique, not dependent on general intelligence or smartness.

The researcher hopes to help people who cannot easily remember faces. She says: "Our findings partly explain why some never forget faces, while others misrecognise their friends and relatives frequently." Further research promises to help people with social disorders like prosopagnosia (face blindness) and autism (developmental disability with impaired communication). If we realise that the mind receives a face as one whole thing and not as a collection of individual parts, "we may train people on holistic processing to improve their ability in recognising faces" (cited in Association for Psychological Science 2011).

What is true about the face, that it is recognised holistically and not analytically, is also true of aesthetics. May be we can say the same thing about spiritual vision. Being able to have a spiritual experience is to face reality holistically. It is much more than the sum of the individual parts observed analytically. Spiritual openness is the ability to perceive reality in an integrated, comprehensive and a deeper way.

13

Human Face is the Source of Respect

We meet so many people every day, on the street or at work. Each face is important to us in different ways. How do we place the faces of people we know? Latest scientific research shows that a specific area in our brains is responsible for processing information about human and animal faces. How we recognise them and how we interpret facial expressions, is achieved by a particular area in the brain.

At Israel's Tel Aviv University, Galit Yovel from the Department of Psychology is trying to understand the mechanisms at work in the face area of the brain. The project, aptly named 'Face Lab', combines cognitive psychology with techniques like brain imaging and electrophysiology and tries to understand how the brain processes information about faces.

In her study, Yovel has found that we are better able to recognise faces when we regularly see and interact with them in meaningful settings. It's as though the face-processing sections of the brain recognises faces holistically, not analytically. She is convinced that how we perceive faces is not totally intuitive. This raises the question of how this information is combined in our brain "to understand how separate face and body areas generate a whole body-image impression" (cited in American Friends of Tel Aviv University 2010).

Additions to our familiar face, such as a beard or glasses, are naturally assimilated into or incorporated into the face recognition gestalt of the brain. Other elements that are irrelevant to facial recognition, such as the chair you're sitting on or the background colour, are also conveniently ignored! This could be the reason fashions in hairstyle and eyewear adds so much to personal appearance. The inability to recognise faces is much more common than what is generally assumed. According to her calculation, about 2 per cent of all people are born with "face blindness", (or prosopagnosia). She hopes her research will enable these people to train themselves, via software and other methods, to better differentiate one face from another – especially when the face is that of a beloved or a close associate.

Yovel began to study the neurological basis of face recognition as a post-doctoral student at the Massachusetts Institute of Technology. As she progresses in her research, she has become more convinced: "In principle, faces are very similar to one another. That's probably why we've evolved these complex and specialised face areas in the brain– so that we can more accurately discriminate among the countless faces we encounter throughout our lives" (American Friends of Tel Aviv University 2010).

These studies, Yovel hopes, will lead to new algorithms that can help computers do a better job of recognising faces, as well as help people who lack this crucial social skill. Her study, published in *Journal of Neuroscience and Human Brain Mapping*, is part of a larger project to explore what makes this highly specialised part of the brain unique. They hope to find practical applications for that information.

The study of face recognition, it is hoped, does more than provide an explanation for embarrassing memory lapses. It can help business executives better match names with faces. More importantly, it can lead to better facial recognition software to identify terrorists or criminals. Similar to faces, bodies are also processed by distinct brain areas.

Thus the ability to recognise faces, though not a unique human feature, is one that is absolutely necessary for our social survival. That this ability is located in the brain and can be improved are insights, which will help us to face each other with more respect. In fact, the human face is the source of respect and makes us responsible to each other. By observing the face we become more respectful and responsible!

14

Evolutionary Roots of Human Prejudice

The tendency to perceive others as "us versus them" isn't exclusively human, but appears to be shared by our primate cousins, according to a study led by Yale researchers and reported in the *Journal of Personality and Social Psychology* (Yale University 2011).

In a series of experiments, psychologist Laurie Santos and her team showed that monkeys treat individuals from outside their groups with the same suspicion and dislike as their human counterparts treat outsiders. This suggests that the roots of human intergroup conflict may be evolutionarily quite ancient.

"One of the more troubling aspects of human nature is that we evaluate people differently depending on whether they're a member of our 'ingroup' or 'outgroup,'" Santos said. "Pretty much every conflict in human history has involved people making distinctions on the basis of who is a member of their own race, religion, social class, and so on" (cited in Yale University 2011)

Santos and her team members studied the rhesus macaques monkeys. In order to assess whether monkeys made the same distinctions between 'ingroup' and 'outgroup' individuals, the researchers used a well-known tendency of animals to stare longer at novel or frightening things than at familiar or friendly things. So, they presented subject monkeys with pictures of monkeys who were either in their social group or from a different group. They found that monkeys stared longer at pictures of other monkeys who were outside their group. This implies that monkeys can spontaneously detect who a stranger is and who a group member is.

Neha Mahajan, a Yale graduate student who headed the project, added: "What made this result even more remarkable is that monkeys in this population move around from group to group." This implies that some of the monkeys who were 'outgroup' were previously 'ingroup'. Both monkeys who transferred groups only weeks earlier or total strangers are considered as outgroups. This suggests that these monkeys are sensitive to who is at present the insider or an outsider, implying flexibility.

Santos and her colleagues then asked whether monkeys evaluated ingroup and outgroup members differently and divided them into "good" or "bad" categories. To find out the answer, the researchers showed monkeys a sequence of photos in which photos of ingroup or outgroup monkey faces were paired with good things or bad things. Then they recorded the time monkeys spent looking at both kinds of sequences. They found that monkeys spent little time looking at sequences that included ingroup faces paired with good stuff like fruits or outgroup faces paired with bad stuff like spiders, suggesting that these two kinds of stimuli are similar.

On the other hand, the monkeys stared longer at sequences in which outgroup individuals were paired with positive objects suggesting that this association was unnatural to them. These results suggest that the distinctions humans make between "us" and "them", the roots of human prejudice, may date back at least 25 million years, when humans and rhesus macaques shared a common ancestor. So the bad news is that "the tendency to dislike outgroup members appears to be evolutionarily quite old, and therefore, may be less simple to eliminate than we'd like to think", Santos said. The good news is that monkeys seem to be flexible about who counts as a group member. "If we humans can find ways to harness this evolved flexibility, it might allow us to become an even more tolerant species" (Yale University 2011).

15

Origins of Empathy in Living Beings

According to a study by neuroscientists at the University of Chicago, there is evidence that empathy drives the behaviour of rodents. In the experiment conducted, rats repeatedly free companions from a restraint, out of pure empathy.

The observation, published December 8 in *Science Daily*, places the origin of empathy much earlier in the evolutionary tree than earlier thought. Though such behaviour has been observed in isolation in animals, the concept had not previously been observed in rodents in a laboratory setting. "This is the first evidence of helping behaviour triggered by empathy in rats," said Jean Decety, a professor of psychology and psychiatry at the university. "There are a lot of ideas in the literature showing that empathy is not unique to humans, and it has been well demonstrated in apes, but in rodents it was not very clear. We put together in one series of experiments evidence of helping behaviour based on empathy in rodents, and that's really the first time it's been seen."

> Can we truly become capable of flowering empathy and compassion for one another?

In the experiments, two rats were placed in a cage. One rat was held in a restrainer device – a closed tube with a door that can be nudged open from the outside. The second rat roamed free in the cage around the restrainer, able to see and hear the other rat. Scientists observed that the free rat acted more agitated when its companion was restrained, compared to its activity when the rat was placed in a cage with an empty restrainer. This response offered evidence of an "emotional contagion". It is the simplest expression of empathy, a frequently observed phenomenon in humans and animals in which "a subject shares in the fear, distress or even pain suffered by another subject" (cited in University of Chicago Medical Center 2011).

In fact the rat's subsequent actions clearly comprised of active helping behaviour, a far more complex expression of empathy. After several daily restraint sessions, the free rat learned how to open the restrainer door and free its companion. Though slow to act at first, once the rat discovered the ability to free its companion, it would take action almost immediately, as reported in *Science Daily* (University of Chicago Medical Center 2011).

Psychology researcher Inbal Ben-Ami Bartal, who devised the experiment, remarked: "These rats are learning because they are motivated by something internal. We're not showing them how to open the door, they don't get any previous exposure on opening the door, and it's hard to open the door. But, they keep trying and trying, and it eventually works."

To check if any other motives were involved, different variations of the experiments were designed. In one of them the free rats were given a choice: free their companion or feast on chocolate. Two restrainers were placed in the cage with the rat, one containing the companion and another containing a pile of chocolate chips. Though the free rat had the option of eating all the chocolate before freeing its companion, the rat was equally likely to free the companion before grabbing the chocolate.

"That was very compelling," said Peggy Mason, professor of neurobiology. She added: "Essentially, helping their cage-mate is on par with chocolate. He can hog the entire chocolate stash if he wants to, and he does not. We were shocked" (cited in University of Chicago Medical Center 2011). Additional preliminary studies suggested that females were more likely to become door openers than males, reflecting the relation of empathy to motherhood.

Empathy that has its beginning in lower primates has not yet realised itself in humans. Spiritual awareness and growth enable us to let this evolutionary trait mature and blossom in ourselves. Can we truly become capable of flowering empathy and compassion for one another?

Mind and Body

16

Decoding the Movies of Our Own Minds

Imagine watching one's own dream next day morning on the computer! Or reading the mind of a coma patient and finding out what he is thinking! With the help of advanced brain imaging and computer simulation, scientists at the University of California (UC), Berkeley, are bringing these futuristic scenarios possibly within the reach of us.

Using functional magnetic resonance imaging (MRI) and computational models, these scientists have succeeded in reconstructing people's dynamic visual experiences. As of now, the technology can only reconstruct approximately movie clips people have already viewed. However, the breakthrough paves the way for reproducing the movies inside our heads that no one else has seen, such as dreams and memories.

"This is a major leap toward reconstructing internal imagery," claims professor Jack Gallant, a UC Berkeley neuroscientist and co-author of the study as reported in *Science Daily* (University of California - Berkeley 2011). He adds: "We are opening a window into the movies in our minds."

The future practical applications of the technology could include a better understanding of what goes on in the minds of people who cannot communicate verbally, such as stroke victims, coma patients and people with neurodegenerative diseases. Such a capability may also lay the groundwork for a brain-machine interface so that people with cerebral palsy or paralysis, for example, can guide computers with their minds. Earlier, the researchers recorded brain activity in the visual cortex while a subject viewed black-and-white photographs. They then built a computational model that enabled them to predict with overwhelming accuracy which picture the subject was looking at. In their present experiment, researchers say they have solved a much more difficult problem by actually decoding brain signals generated by moving pictures.

"Our natural visual experience is like watching a movie," said Shinji Nishimoto, one of the researchers. "In order for this technology to have wide applicability, we must understand how the brain processes these dynamic visual experiences" (University of California - Berkeley 2011). The volunteers watched two separate sets of movie trailers, while measuring blood flow through the visual cortex, the part of the brain that processes visual information. On the computer, the brain was divided into small, three-dimensional cubes known as volumetric pixels.

The brain activity recorded, while subjects viewed the first set of clips, was fed into a computer programme that learned to relate visual patterns in the movie with corresponding brain activity.

Brain activity evoked by the second set of clips was used to test the movie reconstruction algorithm. This was done by feeding 18 million seconds of random videos into the computer programme so that it could predict the brain activity that each film clip would most likely evoke in each subject. "We need to know how the brain works in naturalistic conditions," Nishimoto said. "For that, we need to first understand how the brain works while we are watching movies."

The crucial issue is: Can we analyse the brain and reduce the mental and even spiritual experiences to the brain activities? The instinctive answer of the religionists is to deny such possibility, maintaining that spiritual experiences cannot be reduced to the brain waves. At the same time, the marvellous neurological challenges posed by contemporary technology need to be taken seriously.

17

Brain Wiring and Social Connectivity

According to a recent scientific study by British neurobiologists at Cambridge University, human brains have reached their full physical limit and cannot develop further. Simon Laughlin, the main researcher has claimed that the human brain has achieved its maximum physical capacity and we cannot get any smarter in future, because it requires huge extra energy and oxygen, which our body is not capable of providing. The reason behind the conclusion is that "our brain cells cannot be much smaller than their current physical status. They have reached their optimum position." The theory also says that there is no room for better 'wiring' in the human brain. Here, the term wiring means the inter-connection of the different parts of the brain. More efficient wiring would mean a smarter person. The cleverest people have the best wiring.

According to Ed Bullmore, a professor of psychiatry at Cambridge, "Becoming smarter means improving connections between different brain areas but this runs into tight limits on energy, along with space for the wiring." So our brain is physically well connected and according to these scientists, it has reached its optimal level of functioning. That may be the reason why though the weight of the human brain is only 2% of total body weight, it spends 20% of our physical energy.

It is here that we can move from the physical to the collective or social brain. Daniel Goleman, the author of two bestsellers on 'Emotional Intelligence' has come up with a significant book, *Social*

Intelligence: The Revolutionary New Science of Human Relationships (Goleman 2005 & 2006). Goleman draws from the latest findings in brain science to show that we are "wired to connect." Our relationships and daily interactions with parents, spouses, friends, co-workers, bosses and strangers impact our minds and bodies. The 'neural ballet' that we dance with others signals how much we are designed for sociability. Good relationships act like vitamins and bad ones, like poison. According to Goleman, we "catch" other people's emotions like we catch a cold and toxic relationships cause us to send out hormones that impact biological systems from the heart to our immune cells. As reported in *Science and Spirituality*, Goleman covers a wealth of material and it reflects positively on human spirituality. We have an affinity for empathy, cooperation and altruism and can nurture these life-enriching capacities in ourselves and others. At the same time Goleman is critical of the "social corrosion resulting from technocreep," evident in the increasing isolation of people in our technological society.

He also deals with social intelligence in infants, the importance of resilience in children and the dark side of social intelligence, that is, narcissism and psychopathy. He emphasises the healthy consequences of being a 'people person' and on the value in the workplace of socially conscious bosses. He also studies the popularity and effectiveness of teachers who show warmth and positive regard for students and relates them to social intelligence. In the chapter 'From Them To Us', he suggests the need for recognizing when empathy is extinguished and altruistic impulses are closed off. Goleman concludes that positive things can happen in a world where the social brain acts as "a built-in guidance system for charity, good works, and compassionate acts." It is precisely here that genuine spirituality – warmth for people, compassion for the needy and openness to the others, including the Divine, can collectively be fostered. Then we take biological evolution to the next phase of realising ourselves collectively.

18

The Map of Reality within Our Minds

We do not have access to direct knowledge of reality; rather we have access to perceptions and to a set of beliefs that human society has confused with direct knowledge of reality. To embody this insight, philosopher Korzybski is remembered as the author of the dictum: 'The map is not the territory' (Korzybski 1973). Alfred Habdank Skarbek Korzybski (1879 – 1950) was a Polish-American philosopher and scientist. He is remembered for developing the theory of general semantics. Korzybski's work argued that human knowledge of the world is limited both by the human nervous system and by the structure of language.

He elaborates his insight thus: "A map is not the territory it represents, but if correct, it has a similar structure to the territory, which accounts for its usefulness." What this means is that our perception of reality is not reality itself but our own version of it, or our "map". No two people can have exactly the same map. While we all have similar neurological structure, it functions differently in all of us. This is the basis for our problems in communication when we try to impose our map upon another person. Learning to recognise the structure of another person's map allows us to "see the world through their eyes" and therefore understand and relate to others respectfully and accurately (Korzybski n.d.).

Our maps are created by gathering the data through the five senses. Our senses bring certain aspects of the world to our attention, which go through neurological processes or filters, forming our values, beliefs, capabilities, world-views and life-style. These may be

> Human knowledge of the world is limited both by the human nervous system and by the structure of language.

expressed consciously, but mostly they operate outside our awareness. In fact we don't realise that we can consciously alter them to serve us in better ways. When we pour water through a filter, all the water does not go through. Likewise, as information "pours in" from the outside world, the output (our language and behavior) comes according to what we delete (ignoring "useless" information), distort (sea-lion as lion), and generalise ("all crows are black").

In this scheme of things, generalisation is the basis for the formation of our beliefs. And our beliefs, in turn, confirm the generalisation, often selectively. What we believe about the world is how we interact within it. Most often it is our beliefs which limit us. We have beliefs about spirituality, the world, our capabilities and our environment, right and wrong, what is just and unjust, and whether or not we can change, as Rex Steven Sikes of the IDEA Seminar maintains (Sikes 2001). It is this map that provided us with values. Values are the things we invest our time, money and effort in trying to realise. Examples of some of the values we cherish are: freedom, money, love, honesty and integrity. They are things really important to us, according to the "map" we build for ourselves. And we have very definite criteria or rule structures about how we go about attaining them. That is how maps are important for our moral values and religious vision.

The vital lesson we learn from this for religious and spiritual growth is not to mistake the names and categories we assign to things for the things themselves. Hindus are different from Muslims. But after interacting with them we may notice that some Hindus have more in common with Muslims than with fellow Hindus.

The same is applicable to any organisation or company. The danger lies in getting fixated with the old map. We need to go further. The same may be said of each one of us as individuals: the map I have made of myself is not my identity. Both need constant readjustment, growth and continuous synchronisation.

19

Brain Hardwired to Have More Friends

Two recent studies on our ability to have friends are insightful for spiritual life. The first study by professor Robin Dunbar of the University of Oxford and others suggest that there is a link between the number of friends you have and the size of the region of the brain, which is known as the orbital prefrontal cortex, that is found just above the eyes. The study shows that this brain region is bigger in people who have a large number of friends.

> Religion invites us to make friends even with our enemies, enlarging our brain and widening our spiritual vision.

The study suggests that we need to employ a set of cognitive skills to maintain a number of friends (and the keyword is 'friends' as opposed to just the total number of people we know). These skills are described by social scientists as 'mentalising', or, 'mind-reading', which is a capacity to understand what another person is thinking, that is crucial to our ability to handle our complex social world, including the ability to hold conversations with one another. "Mentalising is where an individual is able to follow a natural hierarchy involving other individuals' mind states," Dunbar said. This study, for the first time, suggests that our competency in these skills is determined by the size of orbital prefrontal cortex in our brains (University of Oxford 2012).

The researchers took anatomical images of the brains of 40 volunteers to measure the size of the prefrontal cortex, the part of the brain used in high-level thinking. Participants were asked to make a list of everyone they had social, as opposed to professional, contact with over the previous seven days. They also took a test to determine their competency in mentalising.

"We found that individuals who had more friends did better on mentalising tasks and had more neural volume in the orbital prefrontal cortex, the part of the forebrain immediately above the eyes. Understanding this link between an individual's brain size and the number of friends they have, helps us understand the mechanisms that have led to humans developing bigger brains than other primate species. The orbital prefrontal cortex of the brain has enlarged dramatically in humans over the last half million years," Dunbar said.

Joanne Powell, from the Department of Psychology, University of Liverpool, along with another co-researcher said, "Perhaps, the most important finding of our study is that we have been able to show that the relationship between brain size and social network size is mediated by mentalising skills. What this tells us is that the size of your brain determines your social skills, and it is these that allow you have many friends" (University of Oxford 2012).Dunbar added, "Our study finds there is a link between the ability to read how other people think and social network size."

Another independent study by researchers at the University College, London, found that the number of 'Facebook friends' a person has and the size of particular brain regions are related. They also indicated that the more Facebook friends a person has, the more 'real world' friends they are likely to have. Thus, there may be a connection between the brain size of an individual and the number of friends he has. In other words, some people are 'hardwired' to have more friends.

Combining both these studies, we can very well say that humans are "hardwired" to have friends – some more and some less. It is such friends that make our human lives bearable and enjoyable. Religion invites us to make friends even with our enemies, enlarging our brain and widening our spiritual vision. It helps us to read the minds of the poor and the underprivileged, and, thus, makes us more compassionate and wholesome. It enables us to be friends with the whole universe!

20

Of Social Networking and Grey Matter

Recently, scientists have found a direct link between the number of 'Facebook friends' a person has and the size of particular brain regions. They also showed that the more Facebook friends a person has, the more 'real-world' friends he or she is likely to have.

The researchers, however, pointed out that what they have found is "a correlation and not a cause", in other words, it is not possible from the data to say whether having more Facebook friends makes the regions of the brain larger or whether some people are 'hardwired' to have more friends. The social networking site Facebook has more than 800 million active users worldwide, among them, about 45 million are in India. The site allows people to keep in constant touch with friends. The size of individual networks vary considerably and the study focused on the size of real-world friends and social networks friends.

Geraint Rees, a Wellcome Trust senior clinical research fellow at the University College London, said: "Online social networks are massively influential, yet we understand very little about the impact they have on our brains." He added that this study can "help us begin to understand how our interactions with the world are mediated through social networks. This should allow us to start asking intelligent questions about the relationship between the internet and the brain" (Wellcome Trust 2011).

The researchers studied brain scans of 125 active Facebook users and compared the size of their network of friends, both online and in the real world. They found a strong connection between the number of Facebook friends an individual has and the amount of grey matter in several regions of the brain. Dr Ryota Kanai, the first author of the study, added: "We have found some interesting brain regions that seem to link to the number of friends we have, both 'real' and 'virtual'. The exciting question now is whether these structures change over time, this will help us answer the question of whether the internet is changing our brains"(Wellcome Trust 2011). Together with examining brain structure, the researchers also examined whether there was a link between the size of a person's online network of friends and their real-world network. Previous studies have looked into this, but only in a relatively small sample sizes.

> Our friends and the external world, both virtual and real, continue to shape our physical brain.

The researchers asked their volunteers questions such as 'What is the total number of friends in your phonebook' and 'How many friends have you kept from school and university days that you could have a friendly conversation with now?' Their responses suggest that the size of their online networks also related to the size of their real world networks. "Our findings support the idea that most Facebook users use the site to support their existing social relationships, maintain or reinforce these friendships, rather than just creating networks of entirely new, virtual friends," said Rees.

Dr. John Williams, Head of Neuroscience and Mental Health at the Wellcome Trust, comments, "We cannot escape the ubiquity of the internet and its impact on our lives, yet we understand little of its impact on the brain. This new study illustrates how well-designed investigations can help us begin to understand whether or not our brains are evolving as they adapt to the challenges posed by social media."

Thus, even today our brain continues to evolve and adjust to the changing environment. Our friends and the external world, both virtual and real, continue to shape our physical brain. So, the change in the physical brain, with its spiritual implications, continues to happen even today!

21

Counting Our Friends

In our age of Facebook, Twitter, Whatsapp and such instant communications media, it is supposedly easy to establish and maintain friendships. We may be tempted to think that the more contacts we have, the better our lives will be. Or else because of better technological and communication facilities, we can be personal and intimate with more people. But, today's scientific insights show another scenario.

The evolutionary anthropologist Robin Ian MacDonald Dunbar suggests that brain size limits our number of close friends. This applies to grooming cliques among apes and internet social networks among humans. Recent studies indicate that our species are incapable of managing an "inner circle" of about 150 friends, popularly called "Dunbar's Number" (Krotoski 2010).

Another theory of Dunbar is that "the rings of our social networks ripple out in factors of three." If we assume five closest friends of relatives in the most intimate circle, a factor of three or 15 or so are there who we have regular contact with. Around three times that number, or 45-50, is the boundary of friends who is truly trusted. Three-fold of this, that is, about 150 friends are the ones who consents to a reciprocal and enduring relationship.

> Trustworthy and enduring friendship, though still rare, do enhance the quality of our lives.

In fact 150 close friends may seem a lot. But let us of think of our Diwalior Christmascard list - 50 cards to 50 couples = 100 friends. "It's the number of people that you know as persons and you know how they fit into your social world and they know how you fit into theirs. They are a group of people to which you have an obligation of friendship," notes BBC correspondent Tom Geoghegen (Geoghegan 2009).

Long ago, Aristotle had maintained that "friends must have eaten salt together." This implies that friends have lived a significant part of their life together. They've sat down and shared meals and the ups and downs of life. "You really have to have mulled over things with them to become really good friends and there's only so many people you can do that with." In other words, "You can have friends because of what you do together or enjoy something together like football or shopping, but they're not as profound friends as those who you love for themselves because of something in their character. And it doesn't matter what you're doing with them, even sitting alone in a room." The author of *The Philosophy of Friendship* (Vernon 2005), Mark Vernon, notes that "friendship help us develop as persons." They are invaluable to our human existence.

There is in fact a biological limit to how many close friends like this we can have and it's probably between five and 12. Mark Vernon adds: "I think this idea that you can have virtually limitless numbers of friends does water down the concept of friendship. I think it's one of those things where less is more."

Paradoxically, another study finds that the number of enduring and close friendship can also boost the bank account. A study of 10,000 US students over a period of 35 years suggests the wealthiest people are those who had the most friends at school. Each extra deep school friend, not the fleeting ones, added 2% to the salary. The researchers concluded that "this was because the workplace is a social setting and those with the best social skills prosper in management and teamwork" (Geoghegan 2009).

Thus, friendships are valuable and to be treasured. Even at this era of instant communication, we just cannot have unlimited number of friends. Our brain is wired to have friends, but limited in number. Trustworthy and enduring friendship, though still rare, do enhance the quality of our lives. The ability to have such enduring relationships makes us rich: financially, psychologically and spiritually.

22

Human Beings Exploit Machiavellian Intellect

Judged by population size and distribution, *Homo sapiens* are clearly the most successful primates. A close second, however, would be rhesus macaques, who have thrived in such diverse environments as mountain forests, dry grasslands or urban setups.

When it comes to their social behaviour, people act more or less like rhesus macaques (*Macaca mulatta*), a type of monkey which shares with humans, the strong tendencies for nepotism and political manoeuvering, according to the research by Dario Maestripieri, a primate behaviour expert.

Maestripieri of the University of Chicago has been studying monkeys for more than 20 years and has written extensively on their social behavior (University of Chicago 2010). These monkeys live in complex societies with strong dominance hierarchies and a long-lasting social bonds between female relatives. Individuals constantly compete for high social status and the power that comes with it using ruthless aggression, nepotism, and complex alliances, including political or sexual alliances. According to Maestripieri, the tactics used by monkeys to increase or maintain their power are not much different from Machiavelli or Chanakya's views.

Alpha males, who control the macaques troop of about 50 members, use threats and violence to hold on to the safest sleeping places, the best food, and access to the females in the group with whom they want to have sex. Like human dictators, intent on holding power, dominant monkeys use frequent and unpredictable aggression as an effective form of threat. Less powerful members of the rhesus macaque group are marginalised and forced to live on the edges of the group's area, where they are vulnerable to predator attacks. "In rhesus society, dominants always travel in business class and subordinates in economy, and if, the flight is overbooked, it's the subordinates who get bumped off the plane," Maestripieri added. "Social status can make the difference between life and death in human societies too."

Our Machiavellian intelligence is not something we can be proud of, but, it may be the secret of our success.

Male macaques form alliances with more powerful individuals. Genuine altruism is rare and, in most cases, only a form of nepotistic behaviour. Mothers help their daughters achieve a status similar to their own. Females act in Machiavellian ways also when it comes to reproduction. They make sure they have lots of sex with the alpha male to increase the chances that he will protect their newborns from other monkeys later.

Struggles for power within a group sometimes culminate in a revolution, where the elite group is suddenly attacked by subordinates. These revolutions result in drastic changes in the power structure. A common enemy unites the whole group.

"What rhesus macaques and humans may have in common is that many of their psychological and behavioural dispositions have been shaped by intense competition between individuals and groups during the evolutionary history of these species," Maestripieri said. "Our Machiavellian intelligence is not something we can be proud of, but, it may be the secret of our success. If it contributed to the evolution of our large brains and complex cognitive skills, it also contributed to the evolution of our ability to engage in noble spiritual and intellectual activities, including our love and compassion for other people" (University of Chicago 2010).

As the author claims, our spiritual activities are the result of intense competition, but, that has not been established yet. Surely, we need more studies to verify this claim. If the claim is found to be true, it is a great challenge for religions.

23

Singing, Dancing and Chanting Synchronously

Studying three traditional societies – the Kung San of Southern Africa, the Andaman Islanders and the Australian Aborigines – who represent, most likely, humanity's most ancient populations, Nicholas Wade in "The Faith Instinct," traces the origin of religion. In all these three societies, religious rituals "involving vigorous, highly emotional, night-long sessions of singing and dancing" are found. Ritualized singing, dancing and chanting produces alterations of consciousness, produce powerful psycho/physical healing.

Matt J. Rosanno, author of *Supernatural Selection: How Religion Evolved* (Rossano 2010), refers to clinical studies in music therapy that have shown that "steady, soothing rhythms used pre-surgically can reduce patient pain and anxiety and promote faster recovery." It is true that rowers pulling together rhythmically as a group have higher pain and exhaustion thresholds compared to those who row alone. Studies have shown that people who move synchronously treat each other with greater cooperativeness and generosity. In short, people who move, sing and work synchronously, in fact, bond together emotionally and reap individual health benefits in the process.

Moving from mere synchrony, it is shown that adding the supernatural further enhances the healing effects. Two recent studies have shown that ritualized meditative practices that include a supernatural element produce stronger psycho/physical effects than purely secular ones.

> Religion adds to the survival value for humans.

In one study, volunteers were randomly assigned to one of the three groups practicing different meditative/relaxation techniques: a group that used a spiritual mantra such as "God is love" or "God is peace," a secular group using a phrase such as "I am happy" or "I am joyful," and a control group that was simply given relaxation training. After two weeks of practice lasting 20 minutes a day for two weeks, subjects were tested on measures of anxiety, mood and pain tolerance that was measured by the amount of time they could keep their hands in water of two degrees Celsius. Those practicing spiritual meditation could keep their hands in water twice as long as the other groups. Additionally, the spiritual group had greater anxiety reduction and mood elevation.

In another related study electric shock was delivered to both devout believers and atheists, who were pre-tested for equivalent levels of pain sensitivity. Subjects were then tested in two sessions where electric shock was administered to the hand while viewing either a religious image or a matched non-religious image. Believers showed a significant increase in pain threshold when viewing the religious image. No such change was observed for atheists. Further, believers showed increased activity in the right ventrolateral prefrontal cortex, an area of the brain involved in the evaluation of pain. No such activity was found among atheists.

These studies show that ritual is good and ritual infused with the supernatural is even better. According to Rossano, our ancestors had discovered this thousands of years ago. They were singing, dancing and chanting together long before anyone conceived of the supernatural. According to his theory, religion was born when already existing social rituals became "supernaturalized" (Rossano 2010).

It is postulated that in the beginning, the supernatural was probably envisioned as just a vague healing force, accessible through a ritually induced altered state of consciousness. By including the supernatural, community rituals that had health and healing effects became religious rituals of healing. The effects were quite real:

anxiety levels were reduced, immune systems were strengthened, pain tolerance was increased, social bonds were reinforced, participants' mental and emotional states were elevated.

Singing, dancing and chanting is life enhancing. Bringing the supernatural into them intensifies the experience and the effect. Such a ritual life fosters community and camaraderie producing measurable emotional and physical benefits, indicating that religion adds to the survival value for humans.

24

Gestures, Thoughts and Action

For some of us it is almost impossible to talk without using our hands. Recent scientific experiments show that gestures seem to be important on how we think and act. In fact, they provide a visual clue to our thoughts and may even change our thoughts by grounding them in action.

Two American scientists Sian Beilock and Susan Goldin-Meadow recently published an article in *Psychological Science (*Association for Psychological Science 2011a). They got volunteers to solve a game in which they have to move stacked disks from one peg to another. After they finished, the volunteers were taken into another room and asked to explain how they did it. There is no way to explain these movements without using hands gestures. Then the volunteers tried the task again, with one trick. For some people, the weight of the disks had secretly changed in such a way that some people had to use both the hands to move the disks.

People who had used one hand in their gestures when talking about moving the small disk were in trouble when they got heavier disks. They took longer to complete the task than did people who used two hands in their gestures–and the more one-handed gestures they used, the longer they took. This shows that how our gesture affects how we think and act. Goldin-Meadow and Beilock suggest that the volunteers had cemented how to solve the puzzle in their heads by gesturing about it and were thrown off by the invisible change in the game.

In another version of the experiment, the volunteers were not asked to explain their solution; instead, they solved the puzzle second time with heavier disks. But moving the disks didn't affect performance in the way that gesturing about the disks did. The people who gestured did worse after the disk weights switched, but the people who moved the disks did not–they did just as well as before. So Goldin-Meadow concludes: "Gesture is a special case of action" (Association for Psychological Science 2011).

Prayer may be seen as thought or contemplation leading us to meaningful action and involvement.

The scientists think that there is a strong corelationship between gesturing and acting "because gesturing about an act requires you to represent that act." We are not just reaching out and handling the thing we talk about; we have to abstract from it, indicating it by a movement of our hands.

According to the scientists, "gestures make thought concrete," bringing movement to the activity that is going on in our mind. They suggest that "gesture may be a more powerful influence on thought than action itself." Their presupposition is that "gesture is a bridge between action and abstract thought." They propose that gestures are simulated action and they are produced as the result of a motor simulation in which speakers simulate an action in terms of the specific effectors and movement patterns needed to reach a desired outcome, as though they themselves were performing the action.

This could be useful in education and prayer. The scientists have been working on helping children to understand abstract concepts in mathematics, physics, and chemistry by using gesture. Even in math where the concepts have little to do with action, gesturing helps children learn–maybe because the gestures themselves are grounded in action.

If this theory is accurate, gestures of respect and reverence we use in prayer has stronger effect on us. Prayer may be seen as thought or contemplation leading us to meaningful action and involvement. Further, prayer with proper gestures will be much more effective in calming us and in leading us to the sublime level of oneness with the larger reality. This leads to action derived from inner freedom and leading to meaningful commitment.

Science and Religion

25

Differing Doubts of Science and Religion

Science is naturally skeptical, initially couched in doubt. The goal in science, however, is to leave a state of doubt or ignorance and, through testing and proof, come to know the truth. Obviously, science is uncomfortable with doubt and attempts to overcome it.

"Doubt might be a stumbling block for science, but it is a stepping stone for faith," writes Victor Udoewa, Professor of Education, George Washington University College, in *The Huffington Post* (Udoewa 2011). In the Judeo-Christian tradition, doubt persists at many crucial points of its history. In the Book of Job, the wise old man loses his family, livestock and health. He struggles with God, crying out for an advocate before God. At the end of the long wresting and arguments, God simply asks Job the questions which Job cannot answer: Where were you when I laid the earth's foundation? Who marked off its dimensions? Who provides food for the raven when its young cry out to God and wander about for lack of food? So, we find, in revelation God remains concealed (Udoewa 2011).

> Religion can appreciate the attempts of science to eliminate doubt and still live with them! For religion, doubt finally indicates the depth of life.

In Exodus, Moses asks God, "What is your name?" The answer given is normally translated "I am who I am." But according to Professor

Udoewa, it is better translated as "I will be howsoever I will be." One understanding is that even in the revelation of God's name, God is still hidden. In other words, God is refusing to be labelled or to be placed in a defining box or confined cabin. God is beyond the definition and so he cannot be controlled or manipulated by humans.

It is wrong to assume that faith in God drives away all doubts. That is why we find contradictory formulations of faith in the same religion. When we ponder deeply, we realise it is not necessary to have a uniform theology to be a member of any religion. This is because the truth or knowledge in our religion is different from the kind, science seeks. In the Judeo-Christian tradition, we are not dealing with truth as a set of explanations that describe reality; truth is not "known," but experienced. It is primarily experienced in the events around us that liberate and make us whole. This might help to see why doubt plays a crucial function in religious traditions, unlike in science. You can have doubt about a profound reality and still be transformed by it! (Udoewa 2011).

That is why the most fundamental religious question 'Does God exist?' can be understood differently by science and religion. It is true that both science and religion are after the same truth. Perhaps there are different ways of answering one question. There is a story of a woman who asked a preacher, "Was there really a talking snake in the Garden of Eden?" The preacher responded, "It doesn't matter. What's important is what the snake said." Likewise, maybe 'Does God exist?' is more the scientific question while 'What has God said?' is more the religious quest. It is true that we can experience God and be transformed by him. And yet, we can have serious doubts as to the source and consequence of that experience. For religion, what is more important is to experience the transformative power present in our lives. While for science the empirical and historical evidences may be more important.

Thus, science attempts to overcome doubt and clarify issues, while religion can playfully dwell in the doubtful uncertainties and still celebrate the beauty and depth of reality. Science has the duty, rightfully, to eliminate ignorance and ambiguities. Religion can appreciate the attempts of science to eliminate doubt and still live with them! For religion, doubt finally indicates the depth of life.

26

Religion is Life's Cosmic Adventure

Professor Raimon Panikkar, one of the greatest scholars of the 20th century in comparative religion, theology and inter-religious dialogue, died on August 26, 2010 at the ripe age of 91. He is known to many people around the world through both his lectures and numerous books. What they heard and read were the arresting reflections of a multi-dimensional person, "who was simultaneously a philosopher, theologian, mystic, priest and poet".

Panikkar, who was born on November 3, 1918, had an Indian Hindu father and a Spanish Catholic mother. He received a conventional Catholic education at a Jesuit high school in Spain before starting his university studies. He earned a doctorate in chemistry and became a Catholic priest. In late 1954, when he was already 36, Panikkar visited India, the land of his father, for the first time. It proved to be a watershed, a decisive reorientation of his interests and views of religion. In India, he experienced Hinduism with its vitality and vigour and he was fascinated by it.

> Christianity approaches Christ in a particular and unique way, informed by its own history and spiritual evolution. But, Christ vastly transcends Christianity.

So, he spent years mastering Hindu thought and experiencing its depth. *The Unknown Christ of Hinduism*, based on his doctoral thesis to the Lateran University in Rome, was textual comparison between Thomas Aquinas and Sankara's interpretation of the

Brahma Sutras. His religion was deepened by his experience of God in nature and human beings.

So, one of his key notions was a "cosmotheandric" vision. Such a vision integrates the cosmic and the human dimensions with the divine, without diminishing one aspect at the cost of the other. In fact, he saw life itself as a cosmotheandric celebration with the human, cosmic and divine dimensions of life being affirmed, reverenced, and brought into deep harmony (Panikkar 1982).

Panikkar's personal life and intellectual conviction helped him to see the absolute necessity for dialogue among various religious traditions. Being deeply rooted in his Christian faith, he creatively embraced other religions.

Like Mahatma Gandhi, he claimed unhesitatingly that Christ was not the monopoly or exclusive property of Christianity. He would regard Christ as the universal symbol of divine-human unity, the human face of God. He would accept that "Christianity approaches Christ in a particular and unique way, informed by its own history and spiritual evolution. But, Christ vastly transcends Christianity."

His openness to other religious and non-religious traditions, based on critical reason and committed experience, made him a multi-dimensional person, sought after by various groups. Towards the end of his life's journey, he would claim: "I left Europe as a Christian, I discovered I was a Hindu and returned as a Buddhist without ever having ceased to be a Christian" (cited in Kärkkäinen 2004: 1).

Religious life for him is an adventure of the cosmic mystery, which is open to all. It is truly an experience of awe that enables the believer to relate to other human beings and nature.

For Panikkar a truly spiritual person is truly open to all – God, World and Human beings – and to different religious, cultural and social traditions. He is critical of everything that dehumanised humans and enslaved nature. At the same time, he is essentially optimistic and hopeful regarding our collective venture, which includes humans and the rest of the cosmos. So, he could easily claim that "Religion is not an experiment, it is an experience of life through which one is part of the cosmic adventure."

27

Science and Religion are Not in Conflict

In an elaborate study, conducted over five years through in-depth interviews with scientists at universities whose fields range from biology and chemistry to social sciences, like political science and economics, dispels the popular belief that science and religion are incompatible.

"When it comes to questions about the meaning of life, ways of understanding reality, origins of the Earth and how life developed on it, many have seen religion and science as being at odds and even in irreconcilable conflict," said Elaine Ecklund, a sociologist from Rice University, Houston. Yet, a majority of the scientists Ecklund and her colleagues interviewed saw both religion and science as "valid avenues of knowledge", she said.

Ecklund (Kaleem 2011)and her team interviewed 275 faculty members from 21 research universities in the United States. Only 15 percent of the respondents said religion and science were always in conflict, while 15 per cent said the two were never in conflict. The majority, 70 per cent, said religion and science are only sometimes in conflict.

Those who were interviewed were selected carefully from broader survey of 2,198 scientists. About half of those in the original survey population said they are identified with a particular religion, while the other half was secular.

"Much of the public believes that as science becomes more prominent, secularisation increases and religion decreases," Ecklund said. "Findings like these among elite scientists, who many individuals believe are most likely to be secular in their beliefs, definitely call into question ideas about the relationship between secularisation and science" (Kaleem 2011).

Ecklund found that the way scientists view the compatibility of religion and science is influenced by how they view religion itself. Scientists who believe the two fields are incompatible are more likely to have a narrow view of religion. Ecklund said scientists who say science and religion are never in conflict often were of the view that "science comes from God, and God created it ... or that science and religion are completely separate ways of viewing reality." In general, those who said religion is compatible with science tended to have a broader view of religion that included non-institutionalised spiritual practices, such as meditation, as Jaweed Kaleem notes in *The Huffington Post* (Kaleem 2011).

For some scientists, a particular type of conservative religion may conflict with science, "but spirituality and other religions are not," asserted the main researcher. She said that scientists who view religion as compatible with their professions are frequently cited as religious scientists as examples of how the two fields can complement each other. Scientists most often spoke highly of Francis Collins, the physician and geneticist who is the director of the National Institutes of Health. Collins has spoken frequently about being a convinced believer and a scientist. He had authored, *The Language of God: A Scientist Presents Evidence for Belief* (2006), where he indicates how his scientific venture is enriched by his religious views, which is in turn got deepened by his scientific outlook.

Most of the pioneers of modern science, including Nicholas Copernicus, Francis Bacon, Galileo Galilei, Rene Descartes, Isaac Newton and Robert Boyle were firm believers. Thus, both science and religion can not only complement each other, but also be spiritual activities that leads us to a deeper experience of life and of the Divine.

28

Faith and Science in Service of Humanity

The two pillars guiding our civilisation are faith and reason. Faith or religion may not always meet reason or science at the theoretical or methodological levels. But, they can meet at other levels. The most successful approach of contact between religions in our country is the practical approach of solving the burning social issues of the country. This can be carried over to the contact with science.

Faith has creed, cult and code. It is at the level of code or praxis that faith and science can converge. Hinduism speaks of the *margas* of *bhakti* (devotion), *jnana* (knowledge) and *karma* (action). It is at the level of *karma* that *bhakti* and *jnana* can converge, at the level of *nishkama karma* or detached action that science and religion can unite.

> Science has distanced itself from wisdom from the period of enlightenment, with its focus on rationality and the subject-object duality. Science tends to treat everything as an object – even people.

Such a convergence can be facilitated by authentic humanism. This is not just one of the significant paths to unifying faith and science, but an essential one. Hence, what can unite the various religions in the country is 'authentic humanism'. The search for 'authentic humanism' will bring out the best in religions and science. Both, science as well as faith are at the service of humanity and profess themselves to be in favour of life, so life would be the meeting point. Faith is concerned with the origin and destiny of humanity, and helps us to transcend and search for a deeper meaning to our lives, thereby making us more human, compassionate, with concern for others. Science is a constant search for knowledge in the quest for making life easier for humanity through harnessing the physical and material resources and using them in the service of humanity.

Faith is at the root of cultures and it imparts moral values that protect and promote social ethics. In India, the focus of religion is often on rituals rather than on social and spiritual values. Religion has to be more self-critical and coherent in practicing the human values it preaches, while science should be at the service of humanity, especially the less privileged and the marginalised who cannot cope up with the pace of scientific changes and, having no access to technological resources, find themselves left behind in the periphery of affluent societies.

One approach to authentic humanism is the return to 'wisdom'– wisdom that applies knowledge to life and sees the deeper meaning of life. Science has distanced itself from wisdom from the period of enlightenment, with its focus on rationality and the subject-object duality. Science tends to treat everything as an object – even people. Objective knowledge gives us a clear idea about 'what is' and provides powerful instruments for the achievement of certain ends. But, it does not provide us with the goal and meaning of life, that is 'what should be', nor does it provide the inspiration for moving towards that goal.

The source of such knowledge and inspiration is wisdom. Wisdom forces us to understand the uniqueness of an individual, while at the same time it teaches us our inter-connectedness, our relatedness. In Indian philosophy, this one-ness is understood as *Advaita*, or the principle of non-duality. *Advaita* deals with understanding reality as a whole, to respect different aspects of reality and to give room for complexity. Thus, there is "differentiation but not necessarily dichotomy," as Professor Francis D'Sa, Director of Institute of Religions, Pune, says (Soares-Prabhu & D'Sa 2001). So, for religion and science to truly serve humanity there is a need for humility. Belief and doubt keep both camps humble. So, serving humanity with humility can be the meeting point for both science and religion.

29

Religion is a Way of Life, Not Just a Theory

Robert Bellah, one of America's most distinguished sociologists, concludes his luminous academic career with the latest book, *Religion in Human Evolution: From the Paleolithic to the Axial Age.* It is a nearly 800-page magnum opus that delves deep into the roots of humankind's encounter with mystery and the search for meaning. Published from Harvard University Press, it is the fruit of 13 years of research and analysis. It has been described as "the most important systematic and historical treatment of religion since Hegel, Durkheim, and Weber. It is a page-turner of a *bildungsroman* of the human spirit on a truly global scale, and should be on every educated person's bookshelves".

Guided by the latest findings in the biological and social sciences, Bellah identifies the roots of the religious sense in human biology and culture– but, by no means reduces religion to a mere expression of biological determinism or cultural preference. In fact, Bellah is all too aware that a big book with the words 'religion' and 'evolution' in the title will strike some as a culture war. He says that both religious and atheistic 'fundamentalists' mistakenly believe that religion and science deal with the same kinds of truth claims and logical system.

"Science operates with a scientific method in terms of which different theories can be tested and proved or disproved, though if

Karl Popper is right, proof is always problematic and we are safer to stick to disproof," Bellah says. "Religion on the other hand, is a way of life more than a theory. It is based on beliefs that science can neither prove nor disprove. Its 'proof' is the kind of person the religious way of life produces."

> Any attempt to make sense of the whole, that situate us in the 'grand design' of things is a religious one.

Religion can be better understood not by examining its statements, but by looking at the way its myths and truth claims are embodied in ritual practice. In the Axial Age – the first millennium BCE, which saw major leaps in religious progress occurring independently, but concurrently in Israel, Greece, India and China – enlightened religious teachers brought a more theoretical approach to myth and ritual, thus, laying the philosophical groundwork for the world's great religious traditions.

"This has led some religious people and many secular people to think that religion is only another form of theory, alongside philosophy and science," Bellah says. "But, while understanding the theoretical achievements of the great traditions is important, we will not really know what they are about, unless, we make the imaginative effort to see how the world might seem if we lived in the embodied practices and narratives of these traditions; a difficult but not impossible task. Indeed, it is the joy of the study of religion to undertake this imaginative task" (Bellah 2011).

Bellah says that anyone who commits to this quest will be in some sense religious. "I was surprised in reading some of the great cosmologists and biologists and finding them express their own response to their work in ways that I could only call religious. Some of them recognised that and some didn't and, perhaps, it would be better in a world of culture wars over religion if those who were speaking beyond science in ways that were to me clearly religious would have recognised that" (Bellah 2011)

Thus, a serious scientific study of religion leads itself to a religious way of life. Religion is not just another form of theory, but one that transforms the world, including the researcher who studies it. In fact, any attempt to make sense of the whole, that situate us in the 'grand design' of things is a religious one.

30

The Grandiosity of Religious Leaders

Religious leaders have power, tremendous power over people. In fact, the spiritual power they exercise over the people cannot be compared to any other modes of exercising power. Precisely therein lies the danger that religious leaders may abuse their power and authority.

> Integrity and authenticity are the hallmarks of spiritual leaders.

Two characteristics of religious leaders who misuse their power are narcissism and grandiosity. The narcissist does not care how uncomfortable he makes the subject, even if the subject expresses or indicates discomfort. That is, an emotionally healthy person would know when another person is feeling uncomfortable. The narcissist does not, or does not care. So he persists in his abusive or domineering behavior. Even after the abuse is revealed, or the abuser is convicted of a crime, the narcissist personality mainly feels sorry for himself.

The abuser with grandiose feelings, is the larger-than-life personality, the frequent lone ranger, who figures into so many abuse narratives. He attracts many followers through the sheer force of his personality. He may even have "unique" characteristics that make him "indispensable". At the same time, he thinks of himself almost like a "mini-god" and precisely therein lies his undoing.

Both of these characteristics – narcissism and grandiosity – are devastating for anyone in religious exercise of power. Yet they are the hallmarks of the abusive and the manipulative religious leader. The temptation of religious leaders is to misinterpret the devotion that ordinary followers have towards them. It is all too human to think that one's charisma and power may even replace that of God! So the greatest danger confronting a "successful" religious leader is to equate his success with God and slowly to equate himself with God.

In fact, narcissism and grandiosity are the very opposites of a spiritual person and even God. A genuine spiritual leader knows that he is not the centre of the world and not even of his own life. Because he knows that greatness comes from God alone, he does not bask under the illusion of his own grandiosity. Therefore, a genuine spiritual person can afford to serve his followers "without counting the cost." He reaches out to them without the need to manipulate them. He leads them to a reality larger than himself. The genuine "masters of spirituality" have shown that it is not by grandiose plan that one experiences God, but humble submission and love that is both "courageous and vulnerable".

Just as love cannot be demanded, worship cannot be coerced. So, activities that are carried out to impress on others cannot have a lasting impact. Thus, a spiritual person becomes attractive when he is devoid of pomposity and undue grandiosity. That is why Indian tradition has always related simplicity and sincerity to spirituality. So, integrity and authenticity are the hallmarks of spiritual leaders.

The task of a genuine spiritual master is to lead the followers not to himself, but to the divine. It is to acknowledge that every human being has his own dignity and self-worth, inalienably given by God. No other human has the right to debase that basic dignity. So, both the leader and the follower surrender themselves to the same God, without bringing any essential difference between them. As Tagore, R." sang, the prayer of a spiritual person is: "Give me the strength never to disown the poor or bend my knees before insolent might." Before God and only before Him can we surrender unconditionally, never before another human person, however grandiose and important he may claim to be!

31

Combining Humility of Intellect and Spirit

Richard Feynman is known as a cheerful eccentric who liked to "play bongos, chase women, and solve advanced problems in theoretical physics." He is one of the most famous physicists of the post-Einstein era. After his studies at the prestigious Massachusetts Institute of Technology and University of Princeton in 1942, he worked during World War II at the Army research centre at Los Alamos, helping design the first atomic bomb of the United States. After the war he became closely associated with the celebrated California Institute of Technology, where he was a professor from 1951 until his death in 1988. He won the Nobel Prize in Physics in 1965 for his work on quantum electrodynamics. Physics students remember him even today for creating a visual representation of subatomic particles and pioneering work in quantum computing.

His first memoir, written in 1985, was quite whimsical, hilarious and anecdotal with the apt title: *Surely You're Joking, Mr Feynman* (Feynman, Leighton & Hutchings 1992). A second Feynman memoir, *What Do You Care What Other People Think?* was published after his death in 1988 (Feynman & Leighton 1988). *The Feynman Lectures on Physics* (Feynman, Leighton & Sands 1963) remain both a popular and classical text in the field even today.

He was both a serious researcher and a jovial human being. Typically, he is not considered a religious man, but a questioner and searcher. That is why his quote on the western civilisation, which we can easily adapt to our Indian culture, is insightful. He holds: "Western civilisation, it seems to me, stands by two great heritages. One is the scientific spirit of adventure – the adventure into the unknown, an unknown which must be recognised as being unknown in order to be explored; the demand that the unanswerable mysteries of the universe remain unanswered; the attitude that all is uncertain; to summarise it – the humility of the intellect. The other great heritage is Christian ethics – the basis of action on love, the brotherhood of all men, the value of the individual – the humility of the spirit" (Feynman 1956). Such an evaluation by an "avowed atheist", as he called himself, is both an opportunity and challenge for religion in contemporary India. For in contemporary India more and more people are naturally turning to logic, beginning to doubt and pose serious questions.

"The humility of the intellect", with its scientific quest and "The humility of the spirit" with its spiritual openness will critique and reinforce each other.

So his comment is: "These two heritages are logically, thoroughly consistent. But logic is not all; one needs one's heart to follow an idea." Then he asks about the place of religion today: "If people are going back to religion, what are they going back to? Is the modern church a place to give comfort to a man who doubts God– more, one who disbelieves in God? Is the modern church a place to give comfort and encouragement to the value of such doubts?" (Feynman 1956).

His ardent desire is that "the humility of the intellect", with its scientific quest and "the humility of the spirit" with its spiritual openness will critique and reinforce each other. These two heritages are the prized possession of contemporary humans. So he asks: "How can we draw inspiration to support these two pillars of western civilisation so that they may stand together in full vigour, mutually unafraid? Is this not the central problem of our time?"

These two heritages drive our human quest forward. Respecting the distinction of these two searches, humans today need to support both these heritages and thus we can shape our collective destiny.

32

Incompatibility of Science and Religion

Recently, *The Huffington Post*, one of the most respected liberal online newspapers, organised a debate on the incompatibility of science and religion. Michael Shermer, founder-editor of *Skeptic* magazine, began his debate by asserting that science "operates in the natural, not the supernatural". He went on to state that "there is no such thing as the supernatural or the paranormal". He concluded his debate by affirming that science provides us with "the best tool ever devised for explaining how the world works, and to work together to create a social and political world that embraces moral principles and yet allows for natural human diversity to flourish".

He maintained that science is the best hope for humanity. "Flawed as they may be, science and the secular Enlightenment values expressed in western democracies are our best hope for survival" (Miller 2012).

The other side represented by Kenneth R Miller, professor of biology, Brown University, started the debate by admitting that often, the word "religion" is identified with those "promoting a frankly anti-scientific view of nature and of our place in the natural world". He admitted that for years, he has fought against these "religiously-motivated efforts to twist, distort, and muzzle science". As a scientist, Brown agrees that "science is a revolutionary activity. It alters our view of nature, and, often, puts forward profoundly unsettling truths that threaten the status quo" (Miller 2012).

Still he urges us to take a deeper look at the relationship between science and religion. The deeper issue, according to Brown is whether there is a genuine incompatibility between science and the concept of God.

What science surely tells us is that the origins of our universe and the creatures in it are found in natural processes that can be observed and studied. This implies that "our own existence is woven into the very fabric of the natural world". This means that human presence is "not a mistake of nature or a random accident, but a direct consequence of the characteristics of our universe". For a believer, God is the primordial source of the profound rationality of nature. Naturally, a non-believer seeks another reason for that rationality because he does not accept God.

> Science is a revolutionary activity. It alters our view of nature, and, often, puts forward profoundly unsettling truths that threaten the status quo.

Even after maintaining and affirming these differences, Brown argues that "both can embrace the systematic study of nature in the project we call science". That is the ultimate source of compatibility between science and religion. Still, there will be conflicts between science and particular religious sects. But a faith that demands "the rejection of scientific reason is not a faith worth having". This view is corroborated by a study on working scientists. A study by Elaine Howard Ecklund and Jerry Z Park conducted in 2009 concluded that "in contrast to public opinion and scholarly publications, most scientists do not perceive there to be a conflict between religion and science" (Miller 2012).

Obviously, science and religion are different ways of thinking, to be sure. "But to insist that conflict is unavoidable is to ignore the common history of science and religion as well as the reality of scientists who see their vocation as perfectly consistent with their faith."

Every human activity, including religion, is in danger of being misguided and needs self-correction, drawn from collective rational critique. The same thing is also true of sciences. By critiquing each other and collaborating for the common good of humanity, science and religion can contribute to our common good. Both science and religion need criticism, on which they should thrive!

33

A Scientist Pope

Contemporary society rightly considers science and religion as autonomous disciplines. But a brief historical retour can throw light on how they can enrich each other, in spite of their legitimate autonomy.

It may be a surprise for many to know that there was a Pope who was an outstanding scientist. Pope Sylvester II (999-1003) known as "the Scientist Pope." He became a Pope "on account of his incomparable scientific knowledge." He was considered by his companions as "acutely intelligent" and "deeply learned in the study of the liberal arts." In fact, he was the leading mathematician and astronomer during the "Dark Ages."

Born in a peasant family of France, Gerbert of Aurillac, who later became Pope Sylvester II, entered a monastery. When he showed extraordinary aptitude for mathematics, his abbot sent him to Barcelona, whose Christian count lived in peace with the Muslim caliph. Since for more than 35 years, the Muslim and Christian kingdoms of Spain lived peacefully, while trade, learning and scientific exchanges flourished. That gave rise to an extraordinarily tolerant culture. For instance, the Islamic Royal Library in Cordoba, on the west of the Great Mosque, contained 40,000 books. By comparison, the greatest Christian library in Europe in those days had only 690 books.

As a professor, Gerbert is the first Christian known to teach mathematics using the nine Arabic numerals and zero which he called "Hindu numerals". Using these new numerals, he devised an abacus, or the counting board, that mimics the algorithms we use today for computing. It has been sometimes called "the first computer".

> The religion that is afraid of science dishonours God and commits suicide (Ralph Waldo Emerson).

Like a modern scientist, Gerbert questioned the authority and performed experiments. He noticed that the math books of his time gave two different methods for finding the area of an equilateral triangle yielding two different solutions. As Nancy Marie Brown, the author of *The Abacus and the Cross: When the Pope Was a Scientist* (2010), notes, Gerbert found the one correct solution leading to scientific enquiry.

So Gerbert was asked to tutor the future king of France and two future Holy Roman Emperors. He become a good friend of them and was convinced that "the power of numbers contained both the origins of all things in itself and explained all from itself" (Brown 2010),

The emperor and the Scientist Pope shared a dream based on peace, tolerance, law and the love of learning. Unfortunately, the emperor succumbed to malaria in 1002 and the Pope a year later.

Because of his extraordinary intelligence, some people branded him as sorcerer. The Church stood with him. In 1602, Cardinal Baronius wrote: "Gerbert was nothing but a learned man who was ahead of his time." In 1999 Pope John Paul II summed up the official church position. Gerbert, he wrote, was "a learned humanist and wise philosopher, a true promoter of culture ... He reminds us that intelligence is a marvellous gift from the Creator" (Brown 2010).

While celebrating the World Year of Astronomy, 2009, Pope Benedict XVI noted that, "Among my predecessors of venerable memory, there were some who studied this science, such as Sylvester II." Further, he added, "The laws of nature which, over the course of centuries, many men and women of science have enabled us to understand better are a great incentive to contemplate the works of the Lord with gratitude."

Thus, it is perfectly legitimate that a learned scientist can truly be a devout religious person. In fact, as the history of Pope Sylvester II shows, it was the wise and the holy people, who first encouraged scientific research and learning. Today, science needs to rediscover its religious heritage and religion needs to dialogue with science on equal terms. "The religion that is afraid of science dishonours God and commits suicide (Ralph Waldo Emerson)."

Truth and Reality

34

Learning to Absorb Truth from the Universe

As already noted Robert Bellah is one of the world's most famous sociologists. The author of *Religion in Human Evolution: From the Paleolithic to the Axial Age* (Bellah 2011a) hopes for a new era of religious awakening.

In the thirteen years he spent working on the book, Bellah has experienced what he calls a "partial conversion". He explains that in order to understand the religions he studied, and the human longings from which they emerged, he had to learn to see the world through the eyes of believers within those traditions and their stories.

"If you spend a lifetime reading and rereading the great dialogues of Plato, as I have done, can you possibly escape being something of a Platonist? And if you immerse yourself in the Pali Suttas of the Buddha can you really avoid not being changed by what you find?" he says. "I think one must have one religious home from which one gets one's most basic orientation, but I see no reason why one can't also learn a great deal from other traditions that perhaps see some things to which your home tradition has not always attended."

Now, at the beginning of the third millennium of the Common Era, Bellah seems hopeful that humankind's religious evolution may be at the beginning of a new Axial Age. This may be an era in which science, a growing

> Christianity and Hinduism overlap in some areas but differ greatly in others

belief in universal human rights, and other features of modernity are leading religious believers the world over to an acceptance that religious pluralism is our common destiny. How is one reconciled to religious pluralism without falling into fundamentalism (the hostile rejection of all religions except one's own) or relativism (the belief that no religion is more true than another)?

The answer, says Bellah, is to resist evaluating the truth or falsity of religions by testing their truth claims, but rather to examine the lives of the people who live by those creeds. By recognising something of worth in the lives and actions of people of other faiths – as the Christian pastor Martin Luther King, Jr., did by looking to the Hindu sage Mahatma Gandhi, for insight into non-violent protest – we may come to understand our own faith in a deeper way. "This is not relativism, nor is it saying all religions are identical," Bellah argues. "Christianity and Hinduism overlap in some areas but differ greatly in others" (Bellah 2011).

"Opening one's self to other religions is always dangerous because you might get converted – that's what we ask of those of other faiths when we live our own in their presence," Bellah says. "What we need to remember is that this is an immense universe, and that there is enough truth to go around without our falling into relativism or losing our grasp on our own tradition. Individuals who hold on to their own faith for dear life and have to deny validity to any other suggest to me that they are deeply insecure and are using their opposition to other faiths to deny the doubts they have about their own" (Bellah 2011).

"Much work is going on now on the evolution of religion, the cognitive science of religion and other kinds of scientific studies," says Paul Wason, Director of Life Sciences at the John Templeton Foundation, USA. "Because Professor Bellah writes from a perspective of the humanities, yet also engages these sciences, his work is uniquely valuable in helping us better understand what religions have actually been like through the millennia." Maybe, the coming together of diverse religions and different sciences will help us to usher a new religious sense. It may open us to a moral consciousness and a new spiritual awareness, leading to a new axial age.

35

You Must Wait for Truth to Come to You

In Indian philosophy 'truth' (*satya*) and 'being' (*sat*) have always been closely associated. So any deep investigation into 'being' should include a phenomenological investigation of'truth'.

The traditional conception of intellectual truth is based on statements or judgements. Here the essence of truth lies in the 'agreement' of the judgment with its object. But what is the nature of this agreement, and what kind of thing is it that connects ideas and ideal things (contents of judgments) with real objects? I know when my judgments are confirmed, that is, when the object shows itself to be as it is asserted to be. Then I know what is intellectual truth.

At a deeper level we can affirm that truth is the occurrence of the discovery of the object through confirmation. So truth is conditioned upon our 'situatedness' or our being-in-the-world.

Some philosophers thus link truth with *aletheia* or disclosedness. This is not merely a definition, but a sign of an ontological feature of human beings. It belongs to the nature of human beings (*Dasein*) to reveal or disclose. In fact, human being is disclosedness and it is to the extent we disclose ourselves that we are.

In this sense, truth belongs uniquely to human beings. Something can be considered 'eternal truth' only to the extent humans can gaze at it, not hold it. Truths, like Newton's Laws, were not true before Newton, which is not to say they were false. They came to be disclosed only through Newton and are true only in their disclosure. Truth, then, "is relative to human beings" though this doesn't mean truth is subjective or relativistic. Thus, we need to humbly bow before the possibility of eternal truth, realising that it is not ours to possess, at least as long as we remain humans.

> You cannot by any process, through any discipline, through any form of meditation, go to truth, God, or whatever name you like to give it. It is much too vast, it cannot possibly be conceived of; no description will cover it, no book can hold it, nor any word contain it. So you cannot, by any devious method, by any sacrifice, by any discipline or through any guru, go to it. You must await it, it will come to you; you cannot go to it.

As to why we presuppose truth and long for it, the answer is our basic human nature. It is our basic humanness to be open to truth and being. It is our basic nature to ask questions and every question points to a level of truth. Truth is the condition of questioning. So total skepticism is as meaningless as total possession of eternal truths. For if we are consistently and totally skeptical, we cannot even raise the question about the nature of our search.

Thus, we are not in full possession of truth, but we can have inklings of it. So, from an Indian perspective, we may claim that truth may be in possession of us. We can truly claim that it is truth that comes to us and not the other way round.

Jiddu Krishnamurthi has a valid insight when he asserts: "You cannot by any process, through any discipline, through any form of meditation, go to truth, God, or whatever name you like to give it. It is much too vast, it cannot possibly be conceived of; no description will cover it, no book can hold it, nor any word contain it. So, you cannot, by any devious method, by any sacrifice, by any discipline or through any guru, go to it. You must await it, it will come to you; you cannot go to it."

All that we can do is be open to the truth. So, he admonishes: "All that the mind can do is be quiet but not with the intention of receiving truth. And that is one of the most difficult things of everyone because we think truth can be experienced right away by doing certain things. Truth is not to be bought any more than love can be bought."

Thus, the truth about truth is that it is a gift over which we have no claim. We would be privileged to be open to it gracefully.

36

Bits of Information that Create Reality

The great 20th century physicist John Archibald Wheeler's phrase, "It from bit" denotes information as the fundamental unit of physics. A bit–or binary digit–is the smallest possible fragment of information. A bit is nothing more than the answer to a "yes-no" question. It has no substance, and yet, taught Wheeler, all physical reality ultimately results from the answers to those questions–meaning, in Wheeler's words, that all physical reality has "an immaterial source and explanation." The universe, therefore, can be thought of as a vast information-processing machine–a computer of the size of the cosmos.

Vlatko Vedral, a 39-year-old professor of quantum information theory at both Oxford University and the National University of Singapore, is emerging as a leading voice among physicists He says that information, and not matter and energy, is the most fundamental building block of reality. It's a radical idea that blurs the line between physics and metaphysics. "I think we are really beginning to understand that we should not think of atoms, of matter and energy, as the fundamental units, but we should really think of bits of information as being the most fundamental entities out of which we can construct everything we observe," says Vedral (Dreher 2011).

In his 2010 book *Decoding Reality*, Vedral takes that concept, one step further, arguing that the universe really ought to be thought of not as a classical computer, but a quantum computer – one in which consciousness plays a role in determining results. In other words, each of us participates in the construction of physical reality. This sort of claim sounds bizarre and shows why quantum mechanics has about it an air of religion. Despite having been confirmed numerous times through experimentation, quantum effects not only defy common sense at the conceptual level but they can only be observed at atomic and sub-atomic levels.

In the June 2011, cover story in *Scientific American*, Vedral contends that the unbridgeable gap between quantum and classical physics is a "myth." He holds: "Until the past decade, experimentalists had not confirmed that quantum behaviour persists on a macroscopic scale. Today, they routinely do." He concludes that, "these effects are more pervasive than anyone ever suspected. They may operate in the cells of our body" (Dreher 2011).

Vedral cites research indicating the quantum process of entanglement may be at work in the navigation systems of robins and in photosynthesis. "The implications of macroscopic objects such as us being in quantum limbo is mind-blowing enough that we physicists are in an entangled state of confusion and wonderment," Vedral concludes in his essay. Earlier, in *Decoding Reality*, Vedral speculated that detecting quantum effects in macroscopic systems provides "hope that one day we may find that nature has already provided us with a quantum computer and all that is left for us to do is to programme it" (Dreher 2011).

As a London undergraduate in the early 1990s, Vedral found his calling when he encountered an astonishing claim in an obscure book: *Information Is Physical.* So, his mission is to devote his scientific career to exploring the implications of that insight. Technology-driven cultural advances over the past two decades have made concepts that were once obscure far more accessible. "We live in the information age," he asserts. Convincing young people that information is "extremely fundamental and important," he says, is a fairly easy task. This has profound religious and social implications.

37

Billions of Planets and Possibilities

It was the famous German philosopher Immanuel Kant who said: "Two things fill me with awe and wonder: the starry skies above me and the moral law within me."

Regarding the starry skies we are discovering still more fascinating facts. New calculations suggest that there may be as many as 60 billion habitable planets just in our own Milky Way galaxy. It may be even more. At least 100 of these planets may be as close as 30 light-years away, writes Ronald Cole-Turner, the H. Parker Sharp professor of ethics at Pittsburgh, US.

Researchers at the European Southern Observatory (ESO) have carefully sampled 102 red dwarf stars in the southern skies. Red dwarfs are very common in our galaxy. Based on its observations and calculations, the ESO team has estimated that approximately 40 per cent of red dwarfs stars are orbited by planets. What's more, these planets are in, what astronomers call, the "habitable zone", meaning they are neither too close nor too far from their "sun". In particular, it means that the temperature may be right for liquid water to exist on the surface of these planets.

The ESO project is the work of an international team using the observations made with the high accuracy radial velocity planet searcher (HARPS). HARPS is a high-precision echelle spectrograph installed in 2002 on ESO's telescope at La Silla Observatory in Chile. "Our new observations with Harps suggest about 40 per cent of all red dwarf stars have a super-earth orbiting in the habitable zone where liquid water can exist on the surface of the planet," says Xavier Bonfils, leader of the team. "Because red dwarfs are so common – there are about 160 billion of them in the Milky Way itself – this leads us to the astonishing result that there are tens of billions of these planets in our galaxy alone," according to Bonfils, as published in the March issue of *Astronomy & Astrophysics* (European Southern Observatory ESO 2012).

The tantalising discoveries of the external world must correspond to the fascinating discoveries of the inner world. Only then can humanity come to terms with themselves. That is the challenge offered by contemporary technology.

"The habitable zone around a red dwarf, where the temperature is suitable for liquid water to exist on the surface, is much closer to the star than the earth is to the sun," says Stephane Udry, another member of the ESO team. Xavier Delfosse, also a member of the ESO team, says, "Now that we know that there are many super-earths around the nearby red dwarfs and we need to identify more of them using both Harps and future instruments. Some of these planets are expected to pass in front of their parent star as they orbit – this will open up the exciting possibility of studying the planet's atmosphere and searching for signs of life" (European Southern Observatory ESO 2012).

What we need urgently is to develop the moral consciousness, echoing Kant's sentiments. At this point, the Indian spirituality and vision can enable us to focus more on the moral or inner life, which I believe, is even more fascinating and multifaceted. Can we explore the almost infinite possibilities opened up by our inner world of moral consciousness? Can we open ourselves to the goodness and beauty in diverse ways leading to more viable ways and infinite possibilities?

Unless we continuously rediscover and refocus on the moral profundity and multiplicity of our inner life, our very survival is at stake. The tantalising discoveries of the external world must correspond to the fascinating discoveries of the inner world. Only then can humanity come to terms with themselves. That is the challenge offered by contemporary technology. Such a response must have an Indian basis, since the British historian affirms, "It is already becoming clear that a chapter, which had a western beginning will have to have an Indian ending if it is not to end in self-destruction of the human race."

38

Human Experience of Time and Future

In its simplest form, time is lucid and clear; linear and non-problematic. Although time itself is not an abstract concept, it is challenging to illustrate time and particularly the future. This is because mental images or static representations of time consistently fail to capture or transmit its true nature. In trying to approach time, it outstrips itself, shedding in its wake the "trace of what it was and for which it is again".

The contemporary philosopher Derrida is insightful when he makes a clear distinction between the future and "*l'avenir*" (to come). He writes: "In general, I try to distinguish between what one calls the future and '*l'avenir*'. The future is that which – tomorrow, later, next century – will be. There is a future, which is predictable, programmed, scheduled, foreseeable. But there is a future, *l'avenir* which refers to someone who comes whose arrival is totally unexpected. For me, that is the real future. That which is totally unpredictable. The Other who comes without my being able to anticipate their arrival. So if there is a real future beyond this other known future, it's *l'avenir* in that it's the coming of the Other when I am completely unable to foresee their arrival."

This meaningful distinction between the future and *l'avenir* helps to think of time as a deep human experience. Why does Derrida call *l'avenir* the real future? According to him, the particular, predictable, programmed, scheduled and foreseeable is merely an image in one's mind. The future one can foresee is the product of one imagination, now. Although these thoughts are referring to the future, they are actually occurring in the mode of being present.

Our commitment and promises are ways of ordering our lives to prepare for the future. As the Jewish philosopher Hannah Arendt asserts: "Promises are the uniquely human way of ordering the future, making it predictable and reliable to the extent that this is humanly possible." In this sense, the significance of the promise is for the present and it carries on to the future.

We should not commit the basic mistake, which is to think of thoughts about the future as the future itself. To visualize the future is more related to the now than the future itself. This is similar to the realisation that our memories are not the same as the past. Memories always occur in the present even though they refer to the past events. Anything I think about the future or the past, presents itself now only as an interpretation thereof, in the mode of being present. *L'avenir* is like nothingness, a positive indeterminate, imminent yet utterly unexpected, an Other that precedes all personal formalities, as Dimitri Hamlin notes in *The Huffington Post*.

Deep down, our experience of the future opens us to the possibility of radical difference and total trust.

A closer look at our experience of time convinces us that time is always experienced as now. This now, however, is never alone. "Now, in the mode of being present, always and already comes together with l'avenir," the totally unexpected and surprising other.

Thus the promise of the future is not the predictable and foreseeable future, but the surprising *l'avenir,* which opens up possibilities to being radically different. It opens us to the other that cannot be manipulated, controlled and possessed by humans. Such a promise of the totally different other is inherent in our experience of time as *l'avenir*. Cautiously and carefully we may relate this Other with God. Deep down, our experience of the future opens us to the possibility of radical difference and total trust. A believer can affirm: "I do not know what my future holds, but I know who holds my future."

39

Meditating without Making any Effort

Meditation is a simple and transformative activity (or non-activity) that makes us feel at home with ourselves. Although, often misunderstood as controlling our mind or stopping our thinking, primarily it is an effortless act, a graceful way of being.

It is a way of being totally present, totally aware with whatever is happening around us. It is being with ourselves completely and nakedly as we are. It is just being aware of thinking, acting, moving or sitting down. Thus, we can have different types of it, such as sitting meditation, sound meditation, walking meditation or being in meditation. In fact, meditation does not demand that we do something purposely. It is just being in the here and now and being aware of it.

Meditation is not against the mind. Nor is it an anti-mind activity. "It is simply that usually the mind is spinning round and round, so it is a stopping of that spin." Such attentive minding of the mind is transformative. It creates an inner spaciousness in which we become aware of the endless "me-centred" dramas of our mind that is like "a drunken monkey leaping from one scenario to another," as Ed and Deb Shapiro, authors of *Be The Change: How Meditation Can Transform You and the World*, writes in *The Huffington Post* (Shapiro & Shapiro 2012).

They elaborate."Meditation can mean really being focused on something, or, it can mean letting go of all focus and simply being still." Meditation is not resolving to do something. It is more like affirming: "I am just going to be here for a moment without doing anything, without following any thought." In such a non-active awareness, there emerges "peace, a surrendering of the mind's activity to this vast silence and spacious awareness" (Shapiro & Shapiro 2012).

Meditation is both an experience of oneness as well as a practice that enables us to be aware of this. When we make friends with ourselves, we discover a freedom from habitual tendencies, from repetitive behaviour, and we experience great joy, peace, and unconditional happiness. It is, therefore, the greatest gift we can give to ourselves, especially, in our hectic lives.

Given all sorts and all manner of distractions, we need some tips, methods or techniques, to remind us to just be still. We need to be guided inward. Therefore, it makes good sense to create a daily practice of meditation, even if it is just for a few minutes. It is better to make meditation an on-going practice. It is also good to meditate for its own sake. Then, we do not have any expectations, causing stress and even a sense of failure, if the expected results do not come about.

As the Shapiros point out, distractions are bound to occur during meditation. It is best to make friends with our "chattering monkey mind" (Shapiro & Shapiro 2012). Merely, naming this monkey mind and befriending it, is the best way to cope with the distractions, which need not be taken very seriously.

Finally, being alone and being at home with ourselves, meditation enables us to be committed to peace. It is a peace that comes out of our own inner depth and enables us to be attentive to the present.

Further, we need to realise that although, there are elaborate techniques of meditation, simple ones are often the most effective. It may begin by taking a deep breath and letting it go. Then, we can be aware of each breath and silently count at the end of each time we breath out, say five, maybe, even recalling our favourite deity. Doing this as many times as we want will help us to settle down, discover peace within and radiate it to the outside world around us. Thus, simple meditation transforms us and the world.

40

Simple but not Easy

For five billion years, life on Earth has evolved ever more complicated means of ensuring survival. Two of these fundamental methods are the basic idea of the self, and the basic drive to satisfy the self's desires. If we didn't have a sense of the ego and the desire to satisfy the ego we would have become extinct long ago.

And yet, the Buddha realized 2,500 years ago that these basic constructions - ego and desire - cause a lot of pain. The ego feels alone. Desires are never satisfied. We always want more. And life just doesn't cooperate; it's just not possible to always keep the pleasant and always avoid the unpleasant. Really, all of us want just a few basic things: success, love, power, meaning, purpose, pleasure. And, of course, none of us want sickness, death, loss, pain, loneliness or grief, as elaborated by J. Michaelson in the *The Huffington Post* (Michaelson 2010).

These basic desires are natural, universal and suffering-creating. In other words, it's the thirst for the fulfillment of these ever increasing desires that causes our misery. All of us feel hunger if we don't eat, and the sensations of hunger are just sensations. But, when we get really hungry and when our hunger is not satisfied, we gradually begin to become angry. There begins misery.

So the conundrum: The needs most fundamental to our biological makeup are also the ones which tend to cause the most suffering. The Buddha gave us the solution. In one of the most unnatural philosophies ever promulgated, he claimed and showed by his own life that it is possible to want less, to be less and with it to be more contended. In great detail, he set forth a way of life with minimal needs and wants and enabling maximal happiness.

We can be deeply involved in the things of the world with a sense of abandonment.

The fundamentals of the teaching is to understand, intuitively and deeply, that *sankharas* - i.e., ideas, emotions people, and everything else - are incapable of providing lasting, happiness. Since they are continuously changing, the joys they bring, even though wonderful or amazing, are short-lived. Even when we achieve exactly what we want, it gets stale after awhile, and we want something else. And, most subtly but also most importantly, *sankharas* (mental formations or dispositions) just happen. There's no one really minding our mental store – it's running on auto-pilot mode. Stimulus, response; cause, effect. "I am angry" implies "Anger has arisen."

The solution is easy to describe and hard to experience: just letting go. Letting go of everything that hinders or binds us. At the later stages of the spiritual path, the letting go becomes quite profound indeed, as it comes to include letting go of everything, even our most insightful thought and consciousness and precious self.

This simple insight is also profound. It is a fundamental reordering of our most basic sense of the world. And so it does take a long time to really sink in. Can I really be equanimous between pain and pleasure, love and its lack? Can I really let go enough so that I can remember, over and over again, that, contrary to all indications, fulfilling my desires will not be as satisfying as lessening them? The path is "simple... but not easy," as noted by Michaelson (2010).

Chasing after our desires and dreams is not the way to happiness, though it may lead to productivity and success. Letting go of them is. This doesn't mean by doing nothing and renouncing everything we become happy. We can feel the rain, raise the children and construct the skyscraper, without chasing, grasping, holding or pushing away things or people. We can be deeply involved in the things of the world with a sense of abandonment.

Towards Greater Authenticity

41

From Anxiety to Authenticity

"Authentic" (*eigentlich*) is one of the favorite expressions of philosopher Martin Heidegger and it means being true to oneself or being genuine. According to this great philosopher, we are born into a world of quiet conformity. Initially everything we do, say, think and believe, have been done, said, thought and believed before. The activities we regard as worthy of our time and effort (learning, work, play), the ultimate values and meanings we pursue (achievement, love, children), and the particular styles and forms through which we pursue these goals have all been provided by our various human cultures. How different our lives are from the lives of ancient "cavemen"!

Unless we find ways to wrest control of our own lives from society, all of our decisions will continue to be made for us by the unnoticed forces of the cultures in which we live. We may not be told which spouse to "choose" or which job to take, but how free are we to reject both marriage and work as basic styles of life? How have we been carried along so successfully by culture without noticing it?

"They" even hide the process by which "they" have quietly relieved us of the "burden" of making choices for ourselves. It remains a complete mystery who has really done the choosing. We are carried along by the "nobody", without making any real choices, becoming ever more deeply ensnared in inauthenticity. This process can be reversed only if we explicitly bring ourselves back from our lostness in the "they". But this bringing-back must have that kind of being by the neglect of which we have lost ourselves in inauthenticity (Park 2006:226-7).

> Returning to this deepest truth of ourselves can bring us back to ourselves and thus we become more authentic.

How can we bring ourselves back from our lostness in conformity? How can we re-possess our lives, wrench ourselves away from the "they"? But if we notice our conformity, inauthenticity, and lostness, perhaps we have the possibility of emerging from our cultural cocoon and creating lives that we clearly own. Initially, we are creatures of our genetic make-up and cultural conditioning. However, in addition to being products of human culture, we are also our powerful and pervasive internal threat-to-being. On this foundation, we can construct our Authentic Existence.

What can reverse the process of sinking deeper and deeper into the "they"? How can we extract ourselves from our conformity, rise above our enculturation? How is it possible to become more whole, centered, and integrated in a world that prevents precisely these qualities from emerging? Beginning as conformists whose "decisions" have already been made by culture, how can we become more unified and focused?

Our existential predicament – or ontological anxiety – is "the rope by which we can climb out of the pit of inauthenticity; it is the handle by which we can grip our own beings"(Park 2006:226-7). First, we must acknowledge our ontological anxiety. This includes peeling away the protective evasions we have so cleverly woven to protect ourselves from the deepest truth of our being. Once we have confronted our ontological anxiety, we must keep it alive, not allow it to die away into comfortable obscurity once again. Instead of letting our being-towards-death fade back into the diversionary small-talk of the "they", we must focus our lives around this "threat". Then our ontological anxiety can become the light of our being – purifying, refining, and integrating our otherwise diffuse, preoccupied and fragmented existence. In the light (or in the shadow) of this constant internal threat-to-being, we are empowered to choose our Authentic projects-of-being. Returning to this deepest truth of ourselves can bring us back to ourselves and thus we become more authentic.

Thus anxiety, when truly listened to, can beckon us to authenticity. Thus, we need to be attuned to our own brokenesss to be blessed!

42

Authenticity Heralded through Yoga

Thomas Berry is a contemporary American environmental mystic and Christian thinker who draws his inspiration also from Yoga and Buddhism. Having penetrated the mystical exuberance of '*samadhi*', the goal of all yoga practitioners, Berry is optimistic about the future of humanity. As noted by William James, the experience of '*samadhi*' grounds an individual in deep-rooted optimism, a surety that, as Julian of Norwich, said, "all will be well, and all will be well, and every kind of thing will be well."

As noted by professor Christopher Key Chapple, Loyola Marymount University, in the US, from his youth, Berry felt a tremendous sense of foreboding, and spoke often of inter-human cruelty through the course of history. He took great pains, for instance, to teach his students about the sufferings inflicted on women in China as their feet were bound, rendering many women immobile and utterly dependent on others. Because Berry is a student of history, he can picture the various kinds of cruelty inflicted by humans on each other (Chapple 1998).

In searching for an answer to the cruelty of human beings, he found in the Buddha, a human being who profoundly articulated the depths of human suffering and taught a way for uprooting and defeating that suffering. Without denying the stuff of human cruelty, and in fact by delving deep into the dark recesses of the mind, reconciliation can be achieved, peace can be found and inhabited. He called upon German philosopher Friedrich Nietzsche in reminding

By examining and knowing suffering as the starting point of the human story, just as Buddha did, Berry suggests that we are able to move more closely to a state of planetary justice.

ourselves that one must "go under" in order to discover that place of authenticity; only in the stark reality of confronting the shadow can be hope for a sense of meaning and peace. One must emerge renewed, heroic and ready to face the challenges of yet a new round of predicaments, including Berry's sad realisation that "the abundance or modern lifestyles comes at a great cost to the world's ecosystems and ultimately threatens the viability of the human".

At a meeting in June 1989 with thinkers and activists, Berry sat late into the night in a heated discussion with Raimundo Panikkar, Jon Sobrino, and Enrique Dussel on the pressing issues of the times. Panikkar, the great Indian thinker, lamented a lack of spirituality and interior life; Sobrino, a Spanish Jesuit activist, bemoaned the horrific injustices being perpetuated by the military juntas in central America; Dussel, an Argentine-Mexican writer and philosopher, advocated that social networks and communities are to be built.

After agreeing with these speakers, Berry suggested that without the context of a sustainable planet earth, no human endeavour would flourish. Drawing from his extensive knowledge of world history, he pointed out that there is no end or beginning to the varieties of unimaginable cruelty that humans have inflicted on each other for millennia. By examining and knowing suffering as the starting point of the human story, just as Buddha did, Berry suggests that we are able to move more closely to a state of planetary justice.

Berry drew from his knowledge of the overarching history of humanity, so he could penetrate and communicate the profound optimism that comes from the connectivity heralded in yoga. As noted by Chapple, these two insights made him realise the great mystery of human suffering. Genuine spirituality confronts the cruelty that we do to ourselves, without becoming hopeless or bitter. It discovers hope and joy from our divine depth and spiritual resources (Chapple 1998).

43

I Envy You

Envy is something we all have to deal with. The philosopher of old, Aristotle understood it "as the pain caused by the good fortune of others." Bertrand Russell, B. said envy was one of the most potent causes of unhappiness. It is a nagging emotion that "occurs when a person lacks another's (perceived) superior quality, achievement, or possession and either desires it or wishes that the other lacked it."

The famous philosopher Immanuel Kant defined it as "a reluctance to see our own well-being overshadowed by another's because the standard we use to see how well off we are is not the intrinsic worth of our own well-being but how it compares with that of others"

Envy can derive from a sense of low self-esteem that results from an upward social comparison threatening a person's self image: another person has something that the envier considers to be important to have. If the other person is perceived to be similar to the envier, the aroused envy will be particularly intense, because it signals to the envier that it just as well could have been he or she who had the desired object.

A recent research published in *Psychological Science*, a journal of the Association for Psychological Science, has found that the fear of being the target of malicious envy makes people act more helpfully toward people who they think might be jealous of them.

Niels van de Ven of Tilburg University and his colleagues Marcel Zeelenberg and Rik Pieters had figured out that envy actually comes in two flavors: benign envy and malicious envy (Association for Psychological Science 2010). They studied people who showed these two kinds of envy and found that people with benign envy were motivated to improve themselves, to do better so they could be more like the person they envied. On the other hand, people with malicious envy wanted to bring down the more successful person. Van de Ven and his colleagues wondered what the experience was like for the people who are the target of the envy.

"In anthropology, they say if you are envied, you might act more socially afterward because you try to appease those envious people," van de Ven maintains, by sharing your big catch of fish, for example.

To prove this, some people were made to feel they would be maliciously envied, by telling them they would receive five Euros – sometimes deserved based on the score they were told they'd earned on a quiz or sometimes totally undeserved. The researchers figured the deserved prize would lead to benign envy, while the undeserved prize would lead to malicious envy. Then the volunteer was asked to give time-consuming advice to a potentially envious person. People who had reason to think they'd be the target of malicious envy were more likely to take the time to give advice than targets of benign envy.

Even envy may serve useful group function, opines van de Ven. We all think people who are better off should share with others, "but that's not something we are inclined to do when we are better off" reports *Science Daily* (Association for Psychological Science 2010). Thus, the fear of envy can encourage us to behave in ways that improve the social interactions of the group.

Still the question remains: Can we truly be happy at the joy of a stranger and of my rival? Buddhism refers to the great virtue of *mudita*, perceving joy in the good fortune of another. This virtue is considered the antidote to envy or *Schadenfreude*. In fact, a spiritual person can see how envy may promote social function. But, *mudita* can do it much better.

44

The Weeds of Life

Over the past 60 years, there has been a dramatic decline in bees in North America, and particularly honey bees, signaling a dire threat to the production of countless food sources. The Guardian reports that four common species of U.S. bumble bees have declined 96 percent in recent decades.

Honey bees have been suffering from the enigmatic colony collapse disorder, and the latest research on U.S. bumble bees only aggravate concerns over food production, as bees are responsible for pollinating 90 percent of the world's commercial plants, from fruits and vegetables to coffee and cotton.

While a correlation between certain fungus infection and the declining bumble bee populations was discovered, the reason is not established. Many think that the growing use of chemical herbicides and pesticides, which are ingested by bees when they make their daily pollination forays, are to blame greatly. The assumption that mobile technology is the cause for it also proved to be wrong. Genetically modified crops, which could be producing pollen with poor nutritional value, is another suspect thought to be responsible for bees disappearing. This theory "is lent credence by the fact that organically raised bees are not undergoing the Colony Collapse Disorder that the other bees are experiencing."

Besides production of honey, bees play a comprehensive and vital role in food production. Plants that depend on bees include apples, almonds, blueberries, peppers, pumpkins, avocados, cucumbers, kiwis, broccoli, alfalfa, cotton, citrus, soya beans, onions, broccoli, carrots, sunflowers, melons, cherries, and many others. Were bees to disappear, most fruits, vegetables, and flowers would disappear with them. Although some crops are pollinated by other insects, birds, bats, or the wind, bees pollinate approximately 80% of all food plants (Loss of Bees Threatens Global Food System 2009).

Other consumables that would be lost without bees would include coffee, tea, and various cooking oils (only olive and walnut would remain). In addition, many common medicines derived from flowering plants, would no longer be available. With the loss of cotton plants, which are also dependent upon bees, there would be no more cotton or denim. Moreover, beeswax, which is used in more than 120 diverse industrial applications ranging from medications and cosmetics to polishes and lubricants, would also disappear. Given that up to 30% of human food supplies rely on bees for pollination, the extinction of bees would result in severe food shortages and devastate economies worldwide (Benjamin & McCallum 2008).

The loss of bees would also mean the loss of other valuable services they can perform. For example, scientists have been using honey bees to detect unexploded landmines, which saves money and, more importantly, human lives. There are a number of things that we can do to help prevent this potential catastrophe.

There are number of things we can do to create bee-friendly spaces. To attract and feed bees. We can plant inexpensive native flowers, berries, fruit trees, and herbs in a garden. We can also grow many different types of plants, since bees, like people, are healthier when they consume a varied diet. Further, we may plant flowers in colours attractive to bees, such as yellow, blue, and purple. Bees don't see the red end of the colour spectrum – red flowers look green, like leaves, to them. Most important, we can learn to set aside a portion of the garden for weeds – particularly white clover, dandelion, milkweed, ironweed, and goldenrod. These are great food sources for bees. Usually weeds bloom when other food sources are disappearing.

I hold that the last point regarding weeds is significant, not only for bees, but also for our own being, for our depth life. We need also time, space and even people, which are not always "cultured, domesticated and refined." Too much of cleanliness, order and regularity is not healthy.

45

Preplaying the Past

Recently scientists have been able to figure out how past experiences influence our behaviour pattern subconsciously. As reported in *Daily Science* (Massachusetts Institute of Technology 2010), scholars at Massachusetts Institute of Technology (MIT) have shown how animals' knowledge obtained through the past experiences can subconsciously programme their behavior for new situations.

Earlier research has indicated when a mouse explores a new space, neurons in its hippocampus, the center of learning and memory, fire sequentially like gunpowder igniting a makeshift fuse. Individual neurons called place cells fire in a specific pattern that mirrors the animal's movement through space. By looking at the time-specific patterns and sequences recorded from the firing cells, researchers can tell which part of the maze the animal was running at the time.

Based on the above data, the new work, conducted by George Dragoi and Susumu Tonegawa, finds that some of the sequences of place cells in mice' brains that fired during a novel spatial experience such as running a new maze had already occurred while the animals rested before the experience.

"These findings explain at the neuronal circuit level the phenomenon through which prior knowledge influences our decisions when we encounter a new situation," Dragoi said. "This explains in part why different individuals form different representations and respond differently when faced with the same situation"(Massachusetts Institute of Technology 2010).

When a mouse pauses and rests while running a maze, it mentally replays its experience. Its neurons fire in the same pattern of activity that occurred while it was running. Unlike this version of mental replay, the phenomenon found by the MIT researchers is aptly termed preplay. It occurred before the animal even started the new maze.

> While relying on intuition and others' wisdom, we need to listen attentively to our own instinctual experiences – shaped genetically and neuronally. They will help us individually and collectively in making decisions that will foster humanity's sustainability and satisfaction.

"These results suggest that internal neuronal dynamics during resting organize cells within the hippocampus into time-based sequences that help encode a related experience occurring in the future," Tonegawa said. Further, he adds: "Previous work largely ignored internal neuronal activities representing prior knowledge that occurred before a new event, space or situation. Our work shows that an individual's access to prior knowledge can help predict a response to a new but similar experience"(Massachusetts Institute of Technology 2010).

The experiment provides us with some information on how we are guided by our past experiences, even when we are unaware of it. At the neuronal level, there is a learning that takes place in us, which allows us to prepare for any future eventualities. In this sense we are hard-wired to learn from our past experiences and our survival is advanced by our prior failures and successes.

It could be possible that such learning may go beyond one individual. Genetically, all humans are interconnected. So, we may be able to locate in our genes and hopefully also in our neuronal networks experiences which further our evolution and survival chances. This could be the preplay that all of us are biologically programmed into.

In India, we may be tempted to relate this to the theory of *karma*. But we should be very cautious to use a nascent scientific discovery to substantiate a philosophical theory. But, we can truly see the interconnectedness – that is both genetic and even neuronal – that may exist among all humans and let us assume, even among all living beings. Are our experiences (individually, collectively and even biologically) collectively pre-playing our responses to new situations, enhancing our survival chance and fulfilment possibility.

So, cold reason and technical know-how alone cannot prepare us for our future, though they have their relative role. While relying on intuition and others' wisdom, we need to listen attentively to our own instinctual experiences – shaped genetically and neuronally. They will help us individually and collectively in making decisions that will foster humanity's sustainability and satisfaction.

46

The Paradox of Placebo Effect

We know that "placebo effect" is synonymous with the power of positive thinking; it works because you believe you're taking a real drug. But, a new study published in *PLOS ONE* and reported by *Health & Medicine* rattles this assumption (Harvard Medical School 2010). Researchers at Harvard Medical School's Osher Research Center and Beth Israel Deaconess Medical Center (BIDMC) have found that placebos work even when administered without the seemingly requisite deception.

Placebos–or dummy pills–are typically used in clinical trials as controls for potentially new medications. Even though they contain no active ingredients, patients often respond to them. In fact, data on placebos is so compelling that many physicians (one study estimates 50 percent) secretly give placebos to unsuspecting patients.

Since such "deception" is morally questionable, Ted Kaptchuk from Harvard Medical School (HMS) teamed up with his colleagues at BIDMC to explore whether or not the power of placebos can be utilised honestly and respectfully (Harvard Medical School 2010).

To do this, 80 patients suffering from irritable bowel syndrome were divided into two groups: the control group received no treatment, while the other group received placebos–which honestly labelled as "like sugar pills"–which they were asked to take twice daily.

"Not only did we make it absolutely clear that these pills had no active ingredient and were made from inert substances, but we actually had 'placebo' printed on the bottle" confirms Professor Kaptchuk. "We told the patients that they didn't have to even believe in the placebo effect. Just take the pills" (Harvard Medical School 2010).

For a three-week period, the patients were monitored. By the end of the trial, nearly twice as many patients treated with the placebo reported adequate symptom relief as compared to the control group (59 percent vs 35 percent). Also, on other outcome measures, patients taking the placebo doubled their rates of improvement to a degree roughly equivalent to the effects of the most powerful medications.

"I didn't think it would work," says an astonished Anthony Lembo, HMS associate professor of medicine at BIDMC. "I felt awkward asking patients to literally take a placebo. But to my surprise, it seemed to work for many of them."

At the same time, the authors caution that this study is small and limited in scope and simply opens the door to the notion that placebos are effective even for the fully informed patient–a hypothesis that will need to be confirmed in larger trials.

Professor Kaptchuk is euphoric, "These findings suggest that rather than mere positive thinking, there may be significant benefit to the very performance of medical ritual. I'm excited about studying this further. Placebo may work even if patients knows it is a placebo."

We may apply this paradox to our belief in God. It has been scientifically established that belief in God makes positive contribution to our physical, mental and spiritual health. Many sceptics regard it as a placebo effect. This is definitely a point of contention between theists and atheists.

If the above experiment is further verified, it may be that praying to God and doing religious activities, even when one thinks they are only a placebo, may be beneficial to humans. According to this study, even if I know that God does not exist and does not care for me, engaging myself with God and performing religious rituals may improve my physical, mental and spiritual state!

If the above experiment could be further validated, it could be that humans are so made that we need placebos – dummy pills or demi-gods! So praying to an unknown or even to a non-existent God may produce results! That is the beauty and paradox of being a human being and a believer in God!

47

There are No Accidents

In the beginning of the New Year 2011 Pope Benedict told the Christians "God's mind was behind complex scientific theories such as the Big Bang, and Christians should reject the idea that the universe came into being by accident" (Pullella 2011).

As reported in *Science Daily*, he continued: "The universe is not the result of chance, as some would want to make us believe," Referring directly to the beginning of universe, popularly called "Big Bang" he said: "Contemplating it (the universe) we are invited to read something profound into it: the wisdom of the creator, the inexhaustible creativity of God."

Though the pope has spoken before about evolution, he has hardly delved back in time to discuss specific concepts such as the Big Bang, which scientists believe led to the formation of the universe some 13.7 billion years ago. At present, scientist at CERN, the nuclear research center in Geneva, have been smashing protons together at near the speed of light to simulate conditions that they believe brought into existence the primordial universe from which stars, planets and life on earth eventually emerged.

Against the atheist assumption that science can disprove God, the Benedict maintained that some scientific theories were "mind limiting" because "they only arrive at a certain point ... and do not manage to explain the ultimate sense of reality." He also admitted that scientific theories on the origin and development of the universe and humans, while not in conflict with faith, left many questions unanswered. Still he could affirm: "In the beauty of the world, in its mystery, in its greatness and in its rationality ... we can only let ourselves be guided toward God, creator of heaven and earth" (Pullella 2011).

> "There are only two ways to live your life. One is as though nothing is a miracle. The other is as though everything is a miracle." So there are no accidents in life: every moment is valuable and gifted. Every person is precious and so a gift to us. Every event is significant and an offer.

The Pope definitely true that for a believer the Big Bang cannot be an accident, but clearly willed by God. In fact, France Anatole would say that "*chance* is the pseudonym *God* uses when He does not want to sign His name."

Normally we would use the word "chance" or "accident" to describe events like Big Bang or the origin of human mans. They are, no doubt, unique or singular events. For a believer it will be a terrible mistake to limit chance or God's actions to such a singular event. In fact slowly from the spectacular the believer comes to the realisation that every moment and everything is willed and sustained by God. Believers will have to accept that even Tsunami that killed so many innocents cannot be a chance or accident. Though they may not fully understand it, God is at work at every moment and in everything, including in evil that we detest so vehemently.

Further, believers and non-believers are called to look around – at the spectacular and ordinary events – and see them as true miracle. The origin of the world is in fact no less a miracle than the gravitational force that keeps the earth on orbit. Once we perceive this miraculous in everything, things attain a magical or mystical property. Both believers non-believers are truly admire the precious life that we possess. More than debating on whether there is a cause for such miracle, we need to focus on the truly miraculous experiences in our day to day events.

Then we can appreciate what Albert Einstein expressed from his mystical consciousness: "There are only *two* ways to live your life. One is as though nothing is a *miracle*. The other is as though everything is a *miracle*." So, there are no accidents in life: every moment is valuable and gifted. Every person is precious and so a gift to us. Every event is significant and an offer.

48

Where Knowledge is Free

On Saturday, January 15, 2011 *Wikipedia*, which started life as an offshoot of *Nupedia*, a free, online encyclopedia being written by experts, celebrated its tenth birthday (Timothy 2005). According to reliable sources, this site already records 410 million unique monthly visitors, making it the fifth most popular site in the world. Wikipedia aims to hit the one billion user mark over the next five years "whilst still maintaining its not-for-profit status," according to its executive director Sue Gardner.

The website's popularity, coupled with its not-for-profit model, has astounded many Silicon Valley players who strive to generate the traffic enjoyed by Wikipedia for monetisation. Gardner said: "We're a little bit confounding to folks in Silicon Valley because they look at us and see the potential for monetisation, just because their entire world is geared toward monetisation." She was categorical when she said: "We don't move in the world of *initial public offerings* and valuation and investment. We never talk about it, we never think about it."

It is also reported that the popular online encyclopedia's in the world would be opening its first oversees office in India and has planned around 80 events across the country to celebrate its 10-year anniversary and broadcast its cause. One of the main reasons Wikipedia setup its overseas office is because India "valued education, free speech and a culture of intellectual debate." It sees India as a high potential country. According to Sue Gardener, executive director of the site, "our main strategic focus right now is on India and other

Can we not really dream of a situation where all humans have free access to knowledge?

countries in the developing world. Massive numbers of people are starting to get connected to the internet, mostly through mobile phones but also through traditional PCs." Besides English, the non-profit organisation will also focus on expanding its database in Hindi and other official Indian regional languages.

Unlike some majors internet giants, Wikipedia chose not to set up servers in China as it did not want the government to interfere in publishing content. "We made a decision that we weren't going to collaborate in our own filtering," confirmed Gardener.

At present, it carries 17 million articles in English – adding more than1,000 new ones everyday – and aims to reach the 50 million target by 2016. There are about 100,000 regulator voluntary contributors to the site. It is based on wikis, open-source software which lets anyone fiddle with a webpage, anyone reading a subject entry can disagree, edit, add, delete, or replace the entry. When the he British journal *Nature* examined a range of scientific entries on *Wikipedia* and *Encyclopedia Britannica*, they found few differences in accuracy.

Two basic principles of Wikipedia are: open-source and voluntary contribution. The term *open* source describes practices in production and development that promote access to the end product's source materials. The full history of the editing of every entry in the encyclopedia can be traced and the author of the article is not given credit. The vast army of more than 300,000 volunteers who have written in more than 250 languages indicates human creativity and generosity in action. If such a vast knowledge resource is achieved in just ten years, it is indeed a credible achievement.

The incredible achievement of Wikipedia invites us to dwell on Tagore, R."'s dream for India: "Where the mind is without fear and the head is held high; Where knowledge is free; Where the world has not been broken up into fragments by narrow domestic walls; Into that heaven of freedom, my Father, let my country awake."

The saga of Wikipedia ignites our hearts and minds. Can we not really dream of a situation where all humans have free access to knowledge?

49

The Silence in the Words

After an arduous and involved conference, involving hours of discussion, the manager thought of Parkinson's law: "Work expands to fill the time available for its completion" (Parkinson's Law1955). Based on a humorous essay published by Cyril Northcote Parkinson in *The Economist* in 1955, this law assumes that work keeps on expanding, to fill the time the committee has at its disposal, an experience commonly shared by many executives.

Its corollaries are: In the computer field: "Data expands to fill the space available for storage." In the economic field: "The demand upon a resource tends to expand to match the supply of the resource." The above law and its corollaries reflect a human dilemma. The more time we have at our disposal, more time we need to spend and vice versa. Somehow, humans are adept at adapting ourselves to keep ourselves over-occupied.

That translates itself from work to talk. In many expert committees and conferences, the cynical experience one has is that the more time we have, we spend it all on talking, rather than on doing. So a cynic may reformulate Parkinson's law to read: "Talk expands to kill the time available."

Whether it be work or talk, one thing, humans are adept at is to fill our time. We cannot really stare at vacuum. We just cannot remain still. We cannot just observe and be. We need to do, talk, react, respond and reflect. Without that most people become paranoid.

That is why it is understandable that we count our own worth by our hectic schedule: the number of people we interact with; the number of things we need to do; the number of committees we head. In fact, the importance of a person is often gauged by how empty or full the appointment dairy is.

> "Spirituality is doing what we do, when we have nothing to do."
> A.N. Whitehead

But, ancient sages have realized that it is not in fact what we do that makes us what we are. What we are is not what we accomplish. What we are, is in fact veiled by our hectic schedule, work or talk. So the typical answer that is proposed is to remain to be less hectic, to work less and to relax more. The model is a typical village, where everyone is happy, since they do not have much to do. They have a lot of time for themselves, it is assumed. And so they are considered close to nature and to their own selves. The villagers are thus idealized and considered as happy, peaceful and contended.

Though there is some truth in this line of thinking, I do not fully buy the argument that the ancients were happier and that the villagers are closer to themselves and to nature. That may be good idealizations, we all need. But, it may not really correspond to the factual situation.

There is no way today's contemporary society can ever think of going back to the "good old days of the past." Talk of such golden days may make us nostalgic, but not spiritual. Spirituality, I believe, is not about returning to the glorious past, but about encountering the depth in the contemporary times: with all its frenzy.

True, genuine spirituality is, as A. N. Whitehead, A. N." said, "Doing what we do, when we have nothing to do." It is also to discover the depth in our hectic routine. It is also to find the "surplus" or feel the tenderness even in the agitated minds and disturbed hearts. It is to live the present, even in its uncontrolled and agitated pace. That is to discover silence (serenity) both in the absence of things (work) and in that of words. It is to find depth in the superficial, experience delight also in the bitter things of life.

50

The Other Side of Silence

Perceptively George Eliot writes in *Middlemarch*: "If we had keen vision and feeling of all ordinary human life, it would be like hearing the grass grow and the squirrel's heartbeat, and we should die of the roar which lies on the other side of silence."

As Rabbi Alan Lurie, in *The Huffington Post* observes, most of us have sometimes in our lives heard this "roar", or perceived the "other side of silence" (Lurie 2010). Mostly it occurs at unexpected moments, may be in between our hectic schedule or in the cave of our hearts. Though felt only momentarily, such "bursting forth" leaves us totally transformed.

Though indescribable, it is in fact a kind of shattering of our daily routine, a kind of dying to our ordinary existence. Such silent and gentle encounters show us that there is a "purposeful presence that underlies all creation, and that there is oneness to everything."

Such moments of experience leads us to identify ourselves with the Existence. It enables us to perceive that there is an Existence which "creates and animates everything, from the squirrel's heartbeat to the spinning of galaxies" (Lurie 2010). Further, we know that through our own consciousness, we can connect to this presence, which is a deeper and truer reality than the one that most of us experience in our everyday lives. Such experiences make our lives truly meaningful. These are the mystical experiences of our everyday life.

As Rabbi Alan Lurie reminds us such a mystical experience, like an aesthetic response to a painting or the pleasures of sexual union, transcends and resists words (Lurie 2010). Still they come out with lame imageries of inadequate metaphors to describe these experiences.

> If we had keen vision and feeling of all ordinary human life, it would be like hearing the grass grow and the squirrel's heartbeat, and we should die of the roar which lies on the other side of silence.

After those experiences, they tell us that our usual experience of reality is in fact dulled, incomplete or even illusory. They also add that this dullness is quite useful, since it is this dullness that protects us from being overwhelmed by the power of the true nature of things.

Mystics yearn to lift this dullness, and to experience the force of life as transparently as possible. In order to experience this, we must penetrate to the "other side of silence". In other words, we must first quiet the constant mental chatter that dulls and distracts us, and once the mind is quieted and there is inner silence we can begin to perceive the "roar" that lies beneath. They offer many techniques to reach out to the other side of silence through meditation, contemplation, *vipassana*, etc. Religions are expected to enable us to such a mystical presence.

They help us to connect with this deeper reality. It can be rightly claimed that such mystical experiences are the original sparks which informs religions. That is why Henri Bergson, the French Philosopher who won the Nobel Prize for Literature in 1921, asserted that"Religion is to mysticism what popularization is to science."

Conversely, mystical experiences are really not limited to the realm of religion. At times such life-transforming experiences do not require the life of pious asceticism or self-abnegation. There have been many instances of "secular mysticism" or "natural mysticism" independent of religious traditions. So, Mahatma Gandhi, affirmed that "God has no religion."

Religion facilitates such an experience. Religions assure us such experiences, however fleeting, are truly present and is available to all of us. Those who have experienced such a connection or oneness with Reality are ready to give up everything for its sake.Paradoxically, we can only wait for such experience. We can never earn it or work our way through it. For such moments of grace are gifted to us. We have no claim to it, just like our own life.

51

Smiles and Stillness can be Contagious

In his simple website, Nipun Mehta, the enterprising, tech-savvy founder of ServiceSpace, raises the basic question: "Who am I?" His answer is insightful: "Since December 31 of 1975, I have been called Nipun Mehta. As such, science tells me I'm 99.9 per cent empty space and 0.1 per cent vibration in constant flux. So, technically, I am seeker of an answer to this very question."

As a high school student Nipun, who was born in Ahmedabad, wanted to either become a tennis progessional or a Himalayan yogi. Instead, by the third year of his computer science and philosophy degree at the University of California, Berkeley, he started his software career at Sun Microsystems. The job there gave him more money than he needed. So, he started to give it away. "As money ran out, I started to give time; and as time ran out, I gave myself."

Dissatisfied by the dot-com greed of the late 90's, Nipun went to a homeless shelter with three friends to "give with absolutely no strings attached." They ended up creating a website, and also an organisation named ServiceSpace. By 1999, those experiments in gifting things and time gave birth to ServiceSpace. It is "an incubator of projects that works at the intersection of volunteerism, technology and gift-economy." What started as an experiment with four friends in Silicon Valley has now grown to a global ecosystem with over 350,000 members that has delivered millions of dollars for service sector gratuitously.

> We need an attitude that brings joy to the others and makes our own heart still. Even the smallest act of kindness, which makes others empowered, enables us to be more rooted and to remain still – emotionally and spiritually.

Over the years, they built thousands of websites for nonprofit organisations and also started incubating a diverse set of charity projects like the DailyGood, the Smile Card and a pay-it-forward rickshaw in India. In 2001, at the young age of 25, Nipun quit his job to become a "full-time volunteer". Then he didn't have a plan of survival beyond six months. In January 2005, Nipun and Guri, his wife of six months, put everything aside to embark on an open-ended, unscripted walking pilgrimage in India, to "use our hands to do random acts of kindness, our heads to profile inspiring people, and our hearts to cultivate truth".

Living merely on a dollar a day, eating wherever food was offered, sleeping wherever a flat surface was available, the couple walked nearly 1,000 kilometres before ending up at a monastery, where they meditated for three months. "That whole year radically deepened the values with which we wanted to carry ourselves," he says. This led both of them to practice small acts of service. The journey continues.

How can we work together? Tag someone with a Smile Card, sit in silence on a particular day, sign up for DailyGood, volunteer on a ServiceSpace project, start a gift-economy endeavour, host public event with everyday heroes, or simply do an act of service that makes you come alive. It is his firm conviction that "in serving others, we'll find ways to stay connected".

So, generosity or "giftivism" has been his driving force that has been championing a "gift economy". He has been deeply influenced by great Indian leaders like Mahatma Gandhi, Vivekananda, Goenka and Krishnamurti. His life of service has been based on his spiritual experiences. So, it is not surprising that this entrepreneur's mission statement in life now reads: "Bring smiles in the world and stillness in my heart."

As reflected through his life experiences, as human beings we do not need many things to be happy and joyful. We need an attitude that brings joy to the others and makes our own heart still. Even the smallest act of kindness, which makes others empowered, enables us to be more rooted and to remain still – emotionally and spiritually.

52

Seeing Through

A mystical experience is a transient and extraordinary experience marked by feelings of unity, harmonious relationship to the Divine and everything that exists. It is accompanied by euphoria, loss of ego functioning, alterations in time and space perception. Normally it is a "unitary experience" that cannot be controlled by one's own will. They are not limited to the religious elite. Even ordinary people experience in their mundane lives. To this effect, the German thinker Karl Rahner speaks of a "mysticism of the marketplace."

The mystical experience is a measurable biochemical phenomenon, notes Rabbi Alan Lurie. This does not diminish or negate its significance, because everything that we experience, from the feeling of love to seeing the mirror in front of us, is some form of biochemical reaction in our bodies. Just as we can explore the tangible qualities of the apple, we can also explore the intangible qualities of love and of the mystical experience.

Mystics know, however, that they have glimpsed only a small part of the whole, because as human beings we are limited by our five senses, our level of development, and our cognitive abilities. As noted by Alan Lurie, their descriptions are remarkably consistent across cultures, times and places, and give us a sense of the qualities of this deeper reality, with the recognition of an omnipresent consciousness that it is the actual "material" of all existence. That is why the 17th Century Jewish philosopher Baruch Spinoza asserted forcefully:

"Besides God no substance can be granted or conceived." That is also the deepest insight of Sankara, when he held that everything we perceive is *maya* or illusion. Albert Einstein, one of the most eminent natural mystics of the last millennium affirmed: "Reality is merely an *illusion*, albeit a very *persistent* one" (Donlan 2009: 47).

All matter originates and exists only by virtue of a force ... We must assume behind this force the existence of a conscious and intelligent Mind.

It is to be noted that when they claim reality as an illusion, they are in no way demeaning or denigrating the world. In fact, the opposite is true. They are asserting that compared to the all pervading Presence, the world is an illusion. As such, the world, together with and connected to the Presence, is sacred and precious.

The contemporary scientists who have ventured deeply in to the essential nature of reality have also seen this Presence. Max Planck, the founder of Quantum Physics, noted: "All matter originates and exists only by virtue of a force ... We must assume behind this force the existence of a conscious and intelligent Mind" (cited in Solomon 2003: 222).

This leads us to have a sense of awe and wonder at our own existence: a sense of the mysterious all around us. Albert Einstein was categorical when he asserted: "The most beautiful thing we can experience is the mysterious. It is the source of all true art and all science. He to whom this emotion is a stranger, who can no longer pause to wonder and stand rapt in awe, is as good as dead: his eyes are closed."

Yes, truly mystical persons are those who are alive and whose eyes are open. They see. They see perceptively and even beyond. In fact they see through the veil. Looking through the daily events and ordinary things they glimpse a grandeur that encompasses us all. Such a Presence, such a Reality is truly fascinating and all embracing. It provides significance for our whole existence.

It must be noted that it is not by denying or denigrating the things of this world that we are able to glimpse this utterly beautiful and blissful Presence. It is by truly seeing through the mundane things of our daily existence that we perceive, though fleetingly, this Presence. Once we perceive this Presence, the things of this world attain radically new meaning and significance.

Evolving Spirituality

53

Sane Spirituality

Radical atheists like Bill Maher, Richard Dawkins, Sam Harris and Christopher Hitchens are on the rise today. Their books are sold in millions, acerbic ads reach many more and lead crusades against religion. Along with them fanatical religious zealots and fundamentalists who proclaim their one God and one way are becoming very powerful politically and financially. Such religious zealots are convinced that their own religion carries the totality of truth and are blind to the larger realities of life: conflicting religious traditions, nuanced human experiences and competing life styles.

In fact, most of us belong to neither of these vociferous and warring camps. Most of us have a "sane spirituality," that recognizes that we are in fact part of a transcendent, divine reality that connect to, or unite with, that infinite ineffable wholeness, which is love, compassion or goodness.

This "diverse, unorganized mish-mash of open-minded and mostly voiceless seekers tends to approach spirituality in a reasonable, rational and even pragmatic manner," claims an American author (Goldberg 2010). Some of us share the world views that are secular and who practice meditation, yoga and other spiritual techniques in order to enhance our well-being. Some others appear to be conventionally religious, in that they attend worship services, celebrate religious holidays and teach our children about our larger religious heritage and remain very open-minded and respectfully receptive to the other traditions.

> The Urge to transcend, to connect deeply, to penetrate the great cosmic mysteries and elevate mundane life to the level of the sacred has always been with us and it always will be.

The sanely spiritual do not suppress their doubts; they think logically and accept the testimony of science. Their likely answer to the query "Do you believe in God?" is, "It depends on what you mean by that term." They are disinterested on debates about an anthropomorphic God. They are comfortable to live with their own doubts and keep on asking questions. In short, they are reasonable individuals who regard the spiritual dimension of life as a central feature of development and pursue it for common good.

This practical, autonomous, experience-driven spirituality recognizes that there are many ways to experience the sacred. It is a down-to-earth antidote to the screaming ideologues and fanatics who falsely polarize religious discussions, claims Philip Goldberg, who has done extensive research on religion in America and has authored *American Veda: How Indian Spirituality Changed the West* (Goldberg 2010a)

It also recognises that spirituality has to show itself in concrete commitments and actions. It is definitely not against belief in a supranational power or life after death. But its focus is primarily on the natural powers that we posses, which can be harnessed for our own betterment. Again its priority is on life before death, so that the countless millions can feel the God who "comes in the form of bread."

It also focuses primarily on the human body, without disregarding the soul. Affirming the dignity of the body, it affirms that the human body is sacred and is to be cared for, owned up and befriended. It perceives the inherent power of the physical body and fosters relationship among human beings, who are primarily physical.

In other words it has different priorities than the religious right, which is focussed on their right doctrines, on their true God and on the life after death. It differs from the militant atheists who claims to know definitely and dogmatically that God and soul do not exist.

Sane spirituality realises that the "urge to transcend, to connect deeply, to penetrate the great cosmic mysteries and elevate mundane life to the level of the sacred has always been with us and it always will be." That impulse, sensibly pursued and sincerely carried out, is the heartbeat of any healthy religion, and the best remedy for the madness of extremism. That is the spirituality of the committed and voiceless majority.

54

True Spirituality Helps us Cope With Life Better

What is happiness and how do we measure it? Recently, the Legatum Institute, a London-based think tank, tried to rank 110 countries for their state of happiness, or the "happiness index". These 110 countries make up 93 per cent of the global population. To measure their relative happiness, they have been evaluated based on eight different categories: Economics, Entrepreneurship, Management, Education, Health, Security, Individual freedom and Social relations (Boiling 2011).

In the evaluation, it was neither the amount of money nor the "quality of life" which was measured. According to the organisers, "The index defines prosperity as both wealth and well-being, and finds that the most prosperous nations in the world are not necessarily those that have only a high gross domestic product (GDP), but are those that also have happy, healthy and free citizens."

What is surprising is that the most "prosperous" nations on earth are dominated by Western Europe. They are in the following order: Norway, Denmark, Finland, Australia, New Zealand, Sweden, Canada and Switzerland, to name a few. What is more surprising is that while China finished at 58, Brazil stood at 45, Russia at 63 and India was remained rather low at the 88th position.

One of the legitimate criticisms against the survey is that it tends to equate happiness with "prosperity" and external freedom.

Still for a country like India, which prides itself as a "spiritual oasis" and a cradle of religions, it makes us retrospect.

It is true that spirituality does not prevent pain and suffering. In fact, most spiritual authors claim the more spiritual a person is, the more one has to go through the "dark night of the soul", which leads to further mental and spiritual darkness.

Thus, although, spirituality does not alleviate human suffering, it makes us cope with life. It provides us with a larger vision and a meaning for our existence. Genuine spirituality liberates us internally and externally so that we can face life with more love and compassion. Thus, true spirituality, even while it does not reduce suffering, enables us to cope with suffering better. It makes us competent to face suffering and sadness, and, thus, cope with them much more effectively. Genuine spirituality does not deny suffering, and, in doing so makes us more free and less anxious. Thus, genuine spirituality and unhappiness cannot go hand in hand.

> If my spirituality is of any worth, it has to enable me to stand up in the long run. It has to enable me to face life, even in its extremes. It has to let me celebrate life with its tragedies. Thus, on the whole, extreme unhappiness and deep spirituality do not go hand in hand.

Liberation, the goal of religions, is not merely the otherworldly. It begins already here on earth. If we continue to be unhappy and unwell, we cannot claim to be religious. If we do not live as "happy, healthy and free citizens", it makes no sense to speak of spiritual maturity or religious openness.

We do not need to take the claims of this survey as an absolute truth. Still, if the survey has some credibility, then it is a warning to India: A land that is the birthplace of four major living religions today, besides numerous minor religions. A land that is spiritually mature and culturally rooted must be, by and large, a happy and contented one. Otherwise, there is something fundamentally wrong with the way we relate to life with our spirituality.

In addition, at a personal level, I may have serious troubles and severe problems. But, if my spirituality is of any worth, it has to enable me to stand up in the long run. It has to enable me to face life, even in its extremes. It has to let me celebrate life with its tragedies. Thus, on the whole, extreme unhappiness and deep spirituality do not go hand in hand. This is true for all people and groups.

55

Spirituality has No Settled Foundations

Raising questions, finding some answers and then, asking more questions are some of the basic human traits. Essentially, we may claim that humans are questioning animals. Professor Sanjai Bhatt from the Delhi School of Social Work summed up this insight when he tersely claimed: "Quest is us."

Bhatt is an academician and a social worker, "committed to bridging the gap between social work education and practice". He experiments with different teaching methodologies and works with grassroots organisations. He is associated with a number of social movements and civil society organisations in various capacities. In his experience with social work, he found that one of the fundamental difficulties with us is that we take the easy way out, accept other's answers and live our lives according to them. Bhatt, who wants "decent work for working people in the organised and unorganised sector", urged all those in the social work profession to look at life seriously and keep on asking fundamental questions, even if they may be disturbing.

He lamented the fact that academicians do not ask the more serious and fundamental questions on life, its goal and its meaning. Many of us are satisfied with the simplistic solutions we have found and persist with those answers, even when the questions have changed. Coming to social workers, although, social work is particularly a practical topic, there is also a need for deep reflection, questioning and moving on.

He was talking at an international conference on "Religion, Spirituality and Social Work" organised by the Centre for Studies in Rural Development, Ahmednagar. Suresh Pathare, director of the centre and the main organiser of the conference, added that there is a necessary connection between religion, spirituality and social work.

In fact, spirituality urges us to question, find some answers and move on. Spirituality does not give us settled foundations on which we can rest on our past laurels or languish in old miseries. Genuine spirituality is not afraid of ambiguities and uncertainties. It cannot stagnate itself with the old answers given by our forefathers.

The easy way out of it is to accept the naïve answers and live as if we have all the answers that we need. Such an attitude leads to fundamentalism and fanaticism.

At the same time, we need to be grateful to the ancient visionaries. The tradition has to be taken seriously but we cannot be enslaved by it. Acknowledging the contribution our forefathers have made and the wisdom they have gained, we need to ask different questions on today's complex life, which poses very different perspectives and challenges. It will be foolish to directly apply the insights of yesterday to today's problems, even at the spiritual realm. The newness of life stems from the human hope that denies the present at every moment. Thus, by raising more questions and seeking more answers, we can organically relate to the traditions of the past. A spirituality that can provide us with challenges and opportunities for the present, based on the past traditions and open to future possibilities, will flourish for the common and collective good of humanity.

A spirituality that can provide us with challenges and opportunities for the present, based on the past traditions and open to future possibilities, will flourish for the common and collective good of humanity.

These sentiments can be well summed up in the beautiful insight of the greatest scientist and mystic of the past century, Albert Einstein: "Learn from yesterday, live for today, hope for tomorrow. The most important thing is not to stop questioning" (cited in Mitchell 2012: ix).

56

Depression in Times of Spirituality

According to a WHO-sponsored study published recently, Indians are the world's most depressed people among the 18 countries with nearly 36 per cent suffering from Major Depressive Episode (MDE), a cluster of symptoms of depression. To be diagnosed with MDE, a subject has to qualify for five out of nine symptoms, which include indicators such as appetite, sleep, mood, lack of concentration and suicidal thoughts (Indians world's most depressed people 2011).

In India, around 9 per cent of people reported to have experienced an extended period of depression within their lifetime and nearly 36 per cent suffer from MDE. The average age of depression in India is 31.9 years compared to 18.8 years in China, and 22.7 years in the US. The study, published in the prestigious *BMC Medicine* journal on July 25, is based on interviews of nearly 90,000 people from 18 different countries. The US, China, Japan, India, Brazil, Mexico, Ukraine and Spain, Germany, Lebanon, Mexico, and South Africa were included in the study.

One in seven people (15 per cent) in high-income countries is likely to get depression over their lifetime, compared with one in nine (11 per cent) in middle- and low-income countries, the study asserts. The study found that people living in wealthier nations like Netherlands, France and the US were less happy and more depressed than those in poorer ones. Netherlands with an average of 33.6 per cent cases of MDE came second while France and the US were placed in third and fourth positions with 32.3 per cent and 30.9 per cent cases respectively. Our neighbouring nation, China, has the lowest MDE incidence: 12 per cent.

MDE is characterised by sadness, loss of interest or pleasure, feelings of guilt or low self-worth, disturbed sleep or appetite, low energy and poor concentration, besides feeling depressed. Women are twice as likely to suffer depression compared to men and the loss of a partner, whether from death or divorce, was a main factor, the study indicates. Depression affects over 120 million people worldwide. It can interfere with a person's ability to work, make relationships difficult, and destroy the quality of life. In some severe cases it leads to suicide, causing 850,000 deaths a year. It may be noted that WHO ranks depression as the fourth leading cause of disability worldwide and projects that by 2020, it will be the second leading cause.

> Sustained depression may indicate the absence of such a bond with the divine. Genuine spirituality enables us to be open to progress, and rooted to our inner self, enabling us to cope with the vagaries of life.

There are some who claim that, strictly speaking, there is no necessary co-relationship between spirituality and depression. There have been some spiritual giants who have suffered both physically and spiritually. Still, spirituality –in its holistic and integral approach – does foster wholeness and well-being. A genuinely spiritual person feels affirmed and accepted by God and the larger reality and such an affirmation must necessarily involve psychological and mental well being.

The prevalence of widespread depression in India is an indication of our lop-sided spirituality and economic progress. We urgently need to realise that spirituality is not merely an individual affair between me and my God. It has to do with the community and with the general well-being of it. We need to rediscover the essential relatedness between physical, economic, psychological and spiritual growth. It would be truly a travesty of religion if Indians, who thrive on religiousness, cannot make their lives more balanced and healthy.

Sustained depression may indicate the absence of such a bond with the divine. Genuine spirituality enables us to be open to progress, and rooted to our inner self, enabling us to cope with the vagaries of life.

57

Honour the Sacred in Every Moment

How many of us rush fast through our days, fall into bed exhausted, and wake up the next morning to do it all over again? For many of us, our lives are composed of millions of moments – mostly meaningless and all strung together – perhaps with a sprinkling of sacred moments mixed in. But, each one of us can think of a few sacred moments in our own life. These are the moments when we are consumed with joy and awe. At these moments, we are fully present. We aren't worrying about tomorrow, or trying to rush through the experience to get to the next. We are in the now, and it is truly amazing.

However, why do we wait for major events to honour these divine moments? Why can't every day, every moment be sacred? Every now? Each moment is sacred – if we decide to make it that way. By honouring every moment, even the "meaningless" ones, we make them sacred.

Honouring the sacred means simply choosing to make each moment precious. It is a tiny shift in perception that gives meaning and importance to each moment. It means stopping to notice the beauty and love around us, and within us. It means being fully present in each moment, because only the present moment truly exists. It means offering every moment to the divine in gratitude. So many of us worry about the future, hold regrets about the past, and completely ignore the present. When we give the now our full attention, even mundane tasks can take on an aura of holiness. Then our lives become millions of meaningful moments. Nothing has changed except our perception, but it makes all the difference.

Imagine living a full, meaningful and joyous life. Imagine miracles happening all around us. Imagine being filled with awe and gratitude each day, and laying down to sleep each night feeling peaceful and relaxed. We can, if we honour the sacred present in us and around us. Thus we make our lives collectively precious.

So, how do we change our perception to that of sacredness? What does it mean to stay in the present moment? Let's see an example: washing dishes. When most of us wash dishes, we hurry through it, often thinking about the million other things we need to get done that day. Our minds are scattered all over the place, focusing on everything but what we are doing. Who can blame us? Washing dishes is not the most exciting experience. However, if we choose to make it a sacred experience, we will want to focus on it. We want to take our time and really pay attention to how the water feels on our hands, how the soap cleanses away the grease and grime, and the sense of satisfaction we get as each dish moves from the dirty pile to the strainer, now clean and shiny.

As we give our full attention to washing the dishes, we are not only "doing", we are fully alive and conscious. We are connected to everything, and we are one with everything.

A simple exercise like 'walking meditation' can be a great practice to help you honour the sacred in your own life. Many of us walk for health or recreation, but we can also walk for spiritual awareness. A walking meditation is a slow, focused walk where we give our full attention to each step we take, the feel of our muscles working, our breathing, and even our surroundings. Then we stay focused on the now. Once we experience it, our life will never be the same. So in small works, we can experience God.

Imagine living a full, meaningful and joyous life. Imagine miracles happening all around us. Imagine being filled with awe and gratitude each day, and laying down to sleep each night feeling peaceful and relaxed. We can, if we honour the sacred present in us and around us. Thus we make our lives collectively precious.

58

Propelling through Spiritual Progress

Propel is an acronym for progress, peace and love. According to the vision of "Propel Group," a Chennai-based creative NGO, striving to promote progress through spiritual depth, the cycle of progress starts with love. Today, many communities around the world get debilitated due to the cycle of hate, conflict and loss. This group believes that more hate causes more loss, whereas, more love, based on India's deep spiritual insights, causes more progress.

Propel Global works towards achieving a fundamental shift in the prevalent paradigm of the world, that is a shift from self-centredness to others-centredness, which is an essential criterion for the equitable and holistic development of humanity, based on solid spiritual outlook.

The vision of this group is "to emerge as the leading service provider to catalyse progress by establishing peace through demonstration of proactive selfless love". Therefore, it tries to "deploy a spectrum of pragmatic products and services in a national and international scenario, in order to facilitate equitable development, holistic progress and improvement in the quality of the lives of people".

The group also believes that India has a significant contribution to make to resolve the conflicts the world faces. Just as how globalisation and liberalisation have spread from the west for the betterment of the planet, spiritualisation blossoms from the east to usher love, peace and progress for all. Therefore, it is natural that the inspiration and strength for the mission of Propel Global is drawn from the ethos of Indian spirituality. The twin fountains of the spirit of life (not death) needed in sustaining civilisations come from India. India is where 'ahimsa' (non-violence) was born in 500 BC, the spirit of caring for all creatures; and from India, also comes the ethos of '*Anbe Sivam*' (love is God), dating back to the first century.

The group believes that "only Indian spirituality has the propensity to offer love with non-violence ... because in the Western brand of spirituality, love has always been tainted with violence somewhere or the other".

Indian tradition, on the other hand, can always base itself on non-violence and love through people like Thiruvalluvar, the poet saint of ancient South India, Mahatma Gandhi, M.", the father of the nation, Martin Luther King, an ardent follower of Gandhi and Mother Teresa who have made the world a better place to live in according to their own unique ways.

Yaseva, the founder and director of Propel Global India, is a techno-socio-spiritual entrepreneur working in the area of creative and innovative ways of creating selfless love, expressed through peace and progress by utilising the medium of culture and social enterprise to develop sustainable paradigms for people.

He is also the founder of Unified Progressive Spiritual Academy, which is a socio-spiritual institution based on Indian spiritual foundation of '*ahimsa* and *ahnbu*' (non-violence and unconditional love) and promotes the integration of '*jnanam*' or wisdom, '*bhakti*' (worship) and '*karma*' (work) in order "to bring about the fullness in the lives of individuals who in turn strive to bring about transformation in the society".

Today, we really need entrepreneurs who enhance the quality of life both spiritually and technologically, so that human beings can learn to live as brothers and sisters and in the process experience sustainable development and harmonious living.

Only Indian spirituality has the propensity to offer love with non-violence ... because in the Western brand of spirituality, love has always been tainted with violence somewhere or the other.

59

Pursue Peace as a Quest for Spirituality

How can we account for the "mindless violence of man against man and man against nature?" How can a spiritual person reduce violence and pursue peace? These were the questions taken up by Vijay Pandurang Bhatkar, the architect of the India's Param series of supercomputers, at the keynote address delivered at a conference in Pune on "Towards Peace: Dreams, Dialogue and Dynamics" held in 2010.

In order to create a culture of peace, we need to create value-based individuals, societies, religions and nation states. Bhatkar emphasised that humans cannot hold together without values. According to Bhatkar, some of the fundamental values that are crucial to create a culture of peace are our interdependence and unity in diversity.

He pleaded that we recognise that everything is truly interdependent. We do not exist in isolation whether as individuals or as societies or as nation-states. If we individuals are interdependent, then, we cannot hope to survive by destroying or harming what we are dependent on. "We are all limbs of the same body, and hence, we cannot harm or injure any part of it without affecting the body itself," he said. This interdependence implies that each member is distinct and equally important. "Each element is equally necessary for the whole. Everyone has equal rights to exist and is, therefore, equally entitled to equal opportunities for survival and growth," he said. This leads to the value of reverence for everyone's rights and opportunities.

If we realise our ultimate connectedness to the whole universe and if we perceive unity behind all diversity, then we can let go of our ego and proactively pursue peace and prosperity.

Secondly, he asserted that we must be able to see the unity behind the diversity we experience all around us. The simple maxim for him is: "If we see diversity, it really stems from the unity and if there is unity, it always expresses through diversity." Taking an example from the scientific world, he noted that scientists are trying to unite all forces of the universe through a grand unification theory. In computers, he explains, "We see this unity in all knowledge representation. Everything that we perceive, scripts, graphics, sound images, video, almost everything is represented as just zeros and ones!" This value of unity in diversity can be found in *advaita* philosophy that "talks about the ultimate unity of man, nature and God and the reality of pure consciousness that pervades everything," said Bhatkar, who was awarded a Padmashri, one of the highest civilian recognitions by the government of India, in 2000.

He also recalled that human beings have made great strides in science and technology in the past few centuries. We have unlocked the "secrets of nature and created new technologies such as nuclear technology, space technology, information technology, biotechnology, nanotechnology, and the like." While they have great constructive potential for human development, they have an equally dangerous potential "when the technologies are in the wrong hands and are used in an indiscriminate manner or for gaining control over others". Thus, he concluded that "pursuit of science alone cannot lead to sustainable progress" and peace. So, he advocated that "science must be synthesised with spirituality, which is a universal value of oneness of all beings. The synthesis of science and spirituality can alone lead to the ascent of humans and preservation of our planet." Thus, these two values of interdependence and unity in diversity enable us to work for peace and progress in our world. If we realise our ultimate connectedness to the whole universe and if we perceive unity behind all diversity, then we can let go of our ego and proactively pursue peace and prosperity.

60

Dietary Habits could Harm Our Sweet Tooth

A recent study reports that seven out of 12 related mammalian species have lost the sense of sweet taste. As each of the sweet-blind species eats only meat, the findings demonstrate that a liking for sweets is frequently lost during the evolution of diet specialisation.

A team of researches from Monell Center, Philadelphia, had revealed the remarkable finding that both domestic and wild cats, who are obligate carnivores, are unable to taste sweet compounds due to defects in a gene that controls the structure of the sweet taste receptor.

When the researchers examined sweet taste receptor genes from 12 related mammalian species with differing eating habits, they found taste loss was widespread in the meat-eating species. So, senior author and behavioural biologist at Monell, Gary Beauchamp, comments, "Sweet taste was thought to be nearly a universal trait in animals. That evolution has independently led to its loss in so many different species was quite unexpected."

It was found that the change in the sweet taste receptor gene was closely related to the animals' diets. Some species like the sea lion, fur seal, Pacific Harbour seal, Asian otter, spotted hyena, fossa, and banded lingsang, which are exclusive meat eaters, had developed defective sweet receptor genes. These findings suggest that "diet-related taste loss has happened repeatedly and independently throughout evolution, demonstrating the importance of dietary niche in the structure and function of an animal's sensory system".

Humans have significantly evolved to include also aesthetic, moral and spiritual "tastes". These new tastes have contributed to the well-being of humans as a species and paved the way for human uniqueness and spiritual strength that we witness today.

To further understand the relationship between feeding behaviour and taste function, the researchers next examined sweet and 'umami' or savoury taste receptor genes in two mammals that have "returned" to the sea – the sea lion and the bottlenose dolphin. These animals were selected because they swallow their food whole, suggesting that taste may not play an important role in their dietary selection. As predicted, taste loss was extensive in these animals. Sweet and umami receptor genes were nonfunctional in both, and the dolphin also had nonfunctional bitter taste receptor genes, reports *Science Daily*.

"Different animals live in different sensory worlds and this particularly applies to their worlds of food. Our findings provide further evidence that what animals like to eat – and this includes humans – is dependent to a significant degree on their basic taste receptor biology," said Beauchamp.

"Our findings clearly show that the extra-oral taste receptors are not needed for survival in certain species," notes lead author and molecular biologist Peihua Jiang at Monell Center. "The animals we examined did not have functional sweet, umami, or bitter taste receptors, so it will be important to identify how their functions were replaced throughout the body."

Humans have significantly evolved to include also aesthetic, moral and spiritual "tastes". These new tastes have contributed to the well-being of humans as a species and paved the way for human uniqueness and spiritual strength that we witness today.

But, what these studies suggest is that if we change our lifestyle, or, if we do not use our tastebuds, there is the danger of them disappearing. Imagine a situation if humans lose the aesthetic, moral or even spiritual appeal. The promise that the study provides is that we, including our physical and spiritual tastebuds, are still evolving.

61

Open Up to Dialogue with all Vulnerability

After Marcus Bussey, the famous thinker and futurist, we may understand *sadhana* "as a quest, striving, struggle involving *tapasya*– a sacrificing of one's veil of certainty – and opening up to dialogue via vulnerability and inner reflection". Every spiritual quest is such a *sadhana*. This striving makes our knowledge, including locational knowledge of a standpoint, "not just received and taken for granted but evolving, interpenetrative and emergent".

Considering the contemporary context, professor Anantha Kumar Giri, Madras Institute of Developmental Studies, pleads for a *sadhana* of multi-valued logic and living. As elaborated by him in his talk at Jnana-Deepa Vidyapeeth, Pune, such multi-valued *sadhana* provides a spiritual transformation of our consciousness and liberates us from clinging "to the absolutism of a singular standpoint"

Multi-valued logic, as elaborated by the contemporary Indian philosopher J. N. Mohanty, builds upon multiple traditions of humanity such as the Jain tradition of *Anekantavada* (many paths to truth), and the Gandhian path of non-violence. It emphasises that "every point of view is partly true, partly false and partly undecidable". Giri distinguishes such logic from a dualistic logic where each point of view claims absolutism for itself. Its absolutist claim is accepted at face value (or denied) by the observer as well as the participant. Giri cautions us that "the fields of life, history and society compel us to realise the partial nature of our absolutist claims".

This being the challenging calling of life today, there is "an inescapable pluralisation that calls for cultivation of a multi-valued logic and living where we move beyond our initial standpoints". This urges us to interact with each other, sometimes, even going inside each other. Such a multi-valued logic and living embodies, according to Giri "an art of autonomy and interpenetration where our autonomy is not fixed but transforms itself in the process of mutual interaction and communication".

Genuine spirituality or sadhana, nonetheless, challenges us to understand and cultivate this "quest for beauty, dignity, dialogue and pluralisation in the midst of ugliness, violence and monological absolutism of various kinds.

One important aspect of multi-valued logic is overcoming what Sri Aurobindo calls "egoistic standpoint" of subject positions or position of actors. While one's egoistic standpoint can be more closed, one's standpoint as a self can be much more open. So, Giri distinguishes between the "closed ego" and the "open self". Transformational streams in psychology, sociology, philosophy and spiritual traditions urge us to realise the distinction between the ego and the self. Thus, overcoming our standpoint as that of an ego and cultivating the standpoint of the self helps us to move beyond our own initial standpoints and be open to and embrace the standpoints of others. This contributes to the "pluralisation of our subject positions". Thus, we can realise the "subject position of the self in place of the subject position of the ego". This enables us to overcome positional fixation and to be open to multi-valued logic and living.

In such a collective search, we are open to "aspirations, strivings and struggles to make life and the society more beautiful, dignified and dialogical". Such a quest or *sadhana* is "striving and struggle in our very existent world". This truly forms a part of our lived life. As Giri elaborates, "It is a fragile, ambiguous and uncertain quest."Genuine spirituality or *sadhana*, nonetheless, challenges us to understand and cultivate this "quest for beauty, dignity, dialogue and pluralisation in the midst of ugliness, violence and monological absolutism of various kinds".

62

Challenge of Idolatry of the Written Word

According to some spiritual leaders, currently, we may be witnessing humanity's next rite of passage. They claim that growing up as a species, we are going through the very same process we've all gone through individually. In this very process, the biggest challenge, according to American author Michael Dowd (2012), is the"idolatry of the written word".

As children, we're guided by beliefs making us think the world was made for us. As adults (at least ideally), we're guided by knowledge and we live our lives contributing to others and the world. Indeed, for healthy adults, self-giving becomes one of life's greatest satisfactions. We begin to question the beliefs we are spoon-fed as children. So, the two transformations, from beliefs to knowledge and from self-focus to contribution, is what makes one a mature adult. Dowd believes that humanity is collectively passing through these two transformations. He calls this species-wide rite of passage, the "Evidential Reformation", and believes it is destined to transform how human beings relate to each other and how our religious traditions mature (Dowd 2012).

> Writing down God's words cannot make him silent. He continues to speak.

"The biggest challenge to our maturing as a species, however, is also what has made it possible for us to get this far: literacy," he claims. Modern science, cumulative knowledge, global communications and our present day technology would have been impossible prior to writing.

In our "childhood" as a species – as tribes, then villages, then chiefdoms, kingdoms, then city-states and nations – our main source of guidance came from organised religious beliefs. Shared allegiance to a particular religion "that bridged ethnic and linguistic differences was a crucial factor in the rise of civilizations." Our instinctual heritage as social mammals fosters cooperation at the level of clan or tribe. As Dowd elaborates, in our "adolescence" as a species, we began to question the beliefs, interpretations, and meanings we had inherited. The birth of this new form of collective intelligence occurred when access to powerful new technologies (beginning with the telescope) increased our ability to discern how things are. We then faced the frightening truth that ancient understandings were not the best maps of what is real and meaningful. Traditional religious beliefs, interpreted literally, lost their credibility and sometimes became stumbling blocks to our collective search for peace.

Some spiritually motivated individuals were thrilled at the prospect of participating in this threshold event. In the 19th century, some of them became "natural philosophers", others "scientists" and still others religious reformers. They were the pioneers of "Evidential Reformation".

The main obstacle to religious people wholeheartedly embracing evidence as divine communication, according to Michael Dowd, has been "idolatry of the written word." This occurred "where ancient oral stories became frozen into unchanging scripture – that was then deemed as the foundational locus for discerning priorities, values, right thinking, and right behaviour" (Dowd 2012). This shift from an oral storytelling to the unchanging scripture as the way, wisdom, morality, and a sense of the sacred is generationally passed on, causing strengthening of religions. At the same time, it led to "a profound and now exponentially growing mismatch" between our lives and our religious experiences. This mismatch is between globally shared and empirically tested updates of evolving Divine wisdom versus preference of some religious people for "eternal and never changing God's word". Writing down God's words cannot make him silent. He continues to speak.

63

Moving from Relevance to a World of Resonance

Before he received the prestigious 2012 Templeton Prize for science and religion interaction, the Dalai Lama, said, "We need to move beyond relevance to resonance" (Huffington 2012). He urged us to move beyond the shallows to the depths, beyond the passing novelties of the moment to the echoes of the soul. "We are," he added, "spending money which we don't have on the things we don't want in order to impress the people we don't like."

To find the peace of mind that alone can replace this aimless search, which has led to an epidemic of stress, anxiety, and drugs, the Dalai Lama, is looking to science (specifically neuroscience) to convince an increasingly skeptical and secular society of the need for contemplation and compassion to change the world and ourselves.

In 2005, he wrote in his book, *The Universe in a Single Atom: The Convergence of Science and Spirituality* (Bstan-'dzin-rgya-mtsho 2005), "The great benefit of science is that it can contribute tremendously to the alleviation of suffering at the physical level, but, it is only through the cultivation of the qualities of the human heart and the transformation of our attitudes that we can begin to address and overcome our mental suffering...We need both, since the alleviation of suffering must take place at both the physical and the psychological levels" (Huffington 2012)

In awarding the Templeton Prize to the Dalai Lama, the organizers acknowledged his "engagement with science and with people far beyond his own religious traditions", and the fact that "for the past 25 years, he has focused on the connections between the investigative traditions of science and Buddhism and encouraged serious scientific investigative reviews of, for instance, the power of compassion and kindness and its broad potential to address the world's fundamental problems".

As soon as I wake up in the morning, I shape my mind. The rest of the day, my body, speech, mind are dedicated to others.

Contained within that citation are three themes that are elaborated by Arianna Huffington, president and editor-in-chief of *The Huffington Post* Media Group, "His work combines scientific investigation with religious exploration; his thoughts on compassion; and his techniques for increasing our capacity for it, including, of course, sleep!"

Of course, these three themes are all inextricably bound together. According to the Dalai Lama, science and Buddhist thought have many things in common. "On the philosophical level, both Buddhism and modern science share a deep suspicion of any notion of absolutes. ...Both Buddhism and science prefer to account for the evolution and emergence of the cosmos and life in terms of the complex interrelations of the natural laws of cause and effect. From the methodological perspective, both traditions emphasise the role of empiricism" (Huffington 2012).

The best way to live such a life, in accordance with the wishes of the Dalai Lama, is truly to be inspired by his own life. His approach to life, as noted by *The Huffington Post,* is very simple. "The important thing is that my daily life should be something useful to others," he said. "As soon as I wake up in the morning, I shape my mind. The rest of the day, my body, speech, mind are dedicated to others."

May be, that is what the Dalai Lama, calls the journey from "relevance to resonance." Instead of seeking to impress others and be relevant, we need to resonate within ourselves. Then, we can resonate with the needs of others. In this process, we discover our own authenticity and can dance with the rhythm of nature.

Openness to the Deeper

64

Be Fully Immersed in the Transcendent

Why is it that according to *Nyaya* logic, it is possible to establish the existence of God, while in the Buddhist logical system it is not all that easy? An adequate answer to this question lies in the concept of knowledge of the different systems. They lead to different kinds of understanding of human beings. They also tell us "whether we can prove the existence of God," according to professor John Vattanky, the world's best authority on *Navya-Nyaya*.

Thus *Nyaya* system has as horizon a theory of knowledge that renders possible the discourse about God; it could be asserted that according to *Nyaya*, the 'Absolute' becomes the horizon of all knowledge and, therefore, also of all human activities.

In his professional life Vattanky (1931-), Jnana-Deepa Vidyapeeth, Pune, India, has analysed each sentence and even each word in the *Isvaravada* section of Epistemology of Perception: Gangesa's *Tattvacintamani*. This made him realise the wider implications of the explanations and argumentations in *Nyaya*. Such an understanding of *Nyaya* helped him to develop his own philosophy, which is consistent with his Christian faith and true to his Hindu heritage.

According to this scholar, "A human being can be fully understood only if his metaphysical relation with the Absolute is accepted as a constitutive principle of his very being." In other words, integral humanism demands transcendence. Such a view naturally rejects a purely empiricist understanding of human beings.

This implies that the fullness of being human can be achieved only in and through the transcendent.

This is because the transcendent remains not only at the theoretical level but at the actual plane "as the centre of human beings". Hence, it invests human life with a unique value and significance not confined merely to the world that is experienced by the senses. "It is in and through this world that transcendence operates," according to Vattanky. Therefore, being human is being fully immersed in this world and fully in the transcendent. Hence "to present a humanism without placing the transcendent at its centre is to impoverish human beings; it will be the greatest injustice to them", says Vattanky (2001).

In concrete, what is the nature of this transcendence? In order to appreciate this, Vattanky has developed his original position, based on the Advaita Vedanta of Adi Shankara, especially as interpreted by the late Richard De Smet. De Smet rejects the all too common acosmic or *maya* interpretation of Sankara and asserts that the true nature of the 'Supreme Brahman' is capable of love and grace. Therefore, the highest Brahman is more than a vast ocean of pure consciousness, but in such a way that the simplicity and plenitude and transcendence of the divine are in no way compromised. Thus the absolute is the highest perfection and is also related to us through an *advaitic* relationship. It is clear that non-duality (*advaita*) is read as a doctrine of creation rather than a teaching of illusion.

This Brahman or transcendence can be described in many ways. The negative description differentiates God from all other reals by stating that it is not so (*neti neti*). Such description teaches us that no term or concept can express God properly because of the expressive power of terms and concepts is restricted to the empirical and, hence, it denies all ideas of finitude in God.

65

Inner and Physical Worlds are Linked

Scientists characterise mass extinctions as times when the earth loses more than three-quarters of its living species in a geologically short interval. Five such extinctions have occurred in the past 540 million years. As the March, 2011, issue of the prestigious journal *Nature* reports, a sixth mass extinction may be underway now (Graduate Division Berkely 2011).

The last mass extinction came some 65 million years ago when a comet or asteroid slammed into the Yucatan Peninsula, in modern-day Mexico, causing firestorms whose dust cooled the planet, and an estimated 76 per cent of species were killed, including the dinosaurs. What is particular about our present mass extinction is that it has happened very quickly over a few centuries, and most significantly, it is human-made (Vaughan-Lee2011).

We are slowly, and in some cases reluctantly, waking up to the global ecological disaster of climate change, extinction of species and pollution. However, there is another dimension to this global predicament that we should not ignore. It is not just the outer environment that is at stake but our inner environment and the connection between the two.

While the Indian and other indigenous cultures would look first to the inner in order to understand the outer, this is not a part of our western heritage. And, while Indian spiritual traditions have helped us to understand that personal transformation depends upon inner change, the larger, macrocosmic dimension of these teachings have been mostly overlooked by contemporary culture. Yet, any holistic, spiritual understanding of our present global predicament is very important.

> While acknowledging and appreciating the newly emerging ecological sensitivity, we also need to rediscover our spiritual roots and connectedness to the rest of the physical and spiritual world. Thus, we can respond holistically – spiritually and technologically – to the impending mass extinction that threatens us.

"How can we then 'face the facts' and take real responsibility for our outer situation if we do not know or acknowledge what is happening in our inner environment, in the inner world of our own soul and the soul of the world?" asks the Sufi teacher, Llewellyn Vaughan-Lee (Vaughan-Lee2011).

It should be understood that just as it is our physical acts which affect the outer world and have produced our ecological crisis, it is our consciousness that directly affects the inner world. The inner world is shaped by the consciousness of humanity more than we understand. That is why so many spiritual teachings emphasise the importance of our attitude, the values by which we live. Our attitude or consciousness is a determining factor of our inner world.

It has been suggested that our present ecological disaster comes from our attitude of separation or false ego. Our present culture is focused on the individual and material welfare at the cost of our inter-relationship to the whole. We also separated the physical world from its roots in the sacred. This allowed humanity to abuse and pollute the world in a way that would be unthinkable for any indigenous culture that respects the sacredness of creation.

Thus, along with the good works we do to restore the precarious ecological balance, we also need to refocus on our inner world. Only when our inner world is in balance, can we contribute to the ecological and cosmic balance. Only when we can truly feel at home with ourselves, can we feel at home in and with the cosmos.

More than we realise, our inner world is connected to the physical world. More than we acknowledge, our individual consciousness shapes the collective consciousness of humanity.

While acknowledging and appreciating the newly emerging ecological sensitivity, we also need to rediscover our spiritual roots and connectedness to the rest of the physical and spiritual world. Thus, we can respond holistically – spiritually and technologically – to the impending mass extinction that threatens us.

66

Worry, Intelligence and the Belief in God

Worrying may have evolved along with intelligence as a beneficial trait, according to a recent study by Dr. Jeremy Coplan, professor of psychiatry at the State University of New York and his colleagues. In their research, they found that high intelligence and worry both correlate with brain activity, suggesting that in humans, intelligence may have coevolved with worry (SUNY Downstate Medical Center 2012).

"While excessive worry is generally seen as a negative trait and high intelligence as a positive one, worry may cause our species to avoid dangerous situations, regardless of how remote a possibility they may be," said Coplan. "In essence, worry may make people 'take no chances', and such people may have higher survival rates. Thus, like intelligence, worry may confer a benefit upon the species," he added.

In this study of anxiety and intelligence, patients with Generalised Anxiety Disorder (GAD) were compared with healthy volunteers to assess the relationship between intelligence quotient (IQ) and worry. In a normal group, high IQ was associated with a lower degree of worry, but, in those diagnosed with GAD, high IQ was associated with a greater degree of worry. The correlation between IQ and worry was significant in both the GAD group and the healthy control group. In the former, the more intelligent worry more than the latter.

> More than believing in God, what is still more important is in what kind of God we believe in – a benevolent, compassionate God or a punishing and frightening one! For one becomes (like) the God one worships!

It is generally assumed that excessive worry tends to exist both in people with higher intelligence and lower intelligence, and less so in people of moderate intelligence. It has been hypothesised that people with lower intelligence suffer more anxiety because they achieve less success in life.

In another independent study, researchers at Harvard University-affiliated McLean Hospital have found that those who believe in a benevolent God, tend to worry less and be more tolerant of life's uncertainties than those who believe in an indifferent or punishing God.

The paper, published in the *Journal of Clinical Psychology*, and presented by lead author David H. Rosmarin, assistant psychologist at McLean, at the annual meeting of the American Psychological Association in Washington, DC, urges mental health professionals to integrate patients' spiritual beliefs into their treatment regimens, especially for patients who are religious.

The paper seeks to find a greater understanding of why people worry, reports data from two separate studies. This study, based on 332 subjects of different religious groups found that those who trusted in God to look after them, had lower levels of worry and less intolerance of uncertainty in their lives than those who did not trust in God.

Another independent study consisting of 125 subjects showed that significant increase in trust in God is connected statistically with significant decrease in intolerance of uncertainty, worry and stress. "We had proposed that beliefs about God, both positive and negative, would relate to both worry and intolerance of uncertainty and we found support for our model," Rosmarin said (SUNY Downstate Medical Center 2012).

The two studies show that intelligence, worry and belief in God are connected. More than believing in God, what is still more important is in what kind of God we believe in – a benevolent, compassionate God or a punishing and frightening one! For one becomes (like) the God one worships!

67

Social Interaction and Spiritual Quest

Recently, scientists have proved that the evolution of intelligence and larger brain sizes can be driven by cooperation and teamwork. Their study shed new light on the origins of what it means to be human and how cooperation enhances intelligence. The study was conducted by scientists at Trinity College Dublin and reported in April, 2012 issue of *Science Daily* (Trinity College Dublin 2012).

In the study, researchers constructed computer models of artificial organisms, with artificial brains. They played the classic games, such as the 'Prisoner's Dilemma', which depicts human social interaction. They used 50 simple brains and the brains played against each other in these classic games. Like in every competition in real life, the successful individuals or brains were rewarded or penalised. The best of these individuals were allowed to reproduce and populate the next generation of individuals.

By allowing the brains of these digital individuals to evolve freely, the researchers showed that the transition to cooperative society leads to the strongest selection for bigger brains. It was found that bigger brains essentially did better as cooperation increased. As the digital individuals played and evolved, the researchers studied their strategies and the growth of their brain. The social strategies that emerge spontaneously led to more intelligent brains with more complex memory and power of decision-making. Human-like behaviour, including forgiveness, patience, deceit, teasing and trickery evolved within the game as digital individuals tried to adapt to each other and their social settings.

Questioning our very existence and pondering over our origins make humans unique. This is a religious or philosophical task. To the extent science provides us new clues and insights, we must accept them so that collectively we can journey towards the answers to these fundamental questions.

"The strongest selection for a larger and more intelligent brains, occurred when the social groups were first beginning to start cooperating, which then kicked off an evolutionary Machiavellian arms race of one individual trying to outsmart the other by investing in a larger brain. Our digital organisms typically start to evolve more complex 'brains' when their societies first begin to develop cooperation," explained Andrew Jackson, School of Natural Sciences, Dublin, one of the scientists who is involved in this research (Trinity College Dublin 2012).

Since 1970, it was believed that social interactions triggered the evolution of intelligence. The present study is the first one that mechanistically links decision-making in social interactions with the evolution of intelligence. Another significance of this study is that it makes use of evolutionary models of artificial intelligence to resolve fundamental biological questions. The lead author of the study, Luke McNally, research fellow, Trinity College Dublin, spoke regarding the significance of this study: "Our extraordinary level of intelligence defines mankind and sets us apart from the rest of the animal kingdom. It has given us the arts, science and language, and above all else, the ability to question our very existence and ponder over the origins of what makes us unique both as individuals and as a species."

Therefore, questioning our very existence and pondering over our origins make humans unique. This is a religious or philosophical task. To the extent science provides us new clues and insights, we must accept them so that collectively we can journey towards the answers to these fundamental questions.

In addition, this search demands another kind of intelligence – the moral or spiritual intelligence.

68

Belief in Religion Opens Doors to All

Jimmy Carter, the 39th president of the United States and Nobel Peace Prize recipient in 2002, has recently authored *NIV Lessons from Life Bible: Personal Reflections with Jimmy Carter* (Carter, Hudson& Reckford 2012). As a Christian, Carter sees his political life as an extension of his religious convictions.

In an interview with Paul Brandeis Raushenbush, *The Huffington Post's* senior religion editor, Carter spoke about some of the challenging questions presented in the Bible: from gays, science and the role of women, to name a few (Raushenbush 2012).

To the direct question, "Did God write the Bible?" Carter answered, "God inspired the Bible, but, didn't write every word in the Bible. We know, for instance that stars can't fall on the earth, stars are much larger than the earth. That was a limitation of knowledge of the universe or physics, or astronomy at that time, but, that doesn't bother me at all."

Regarding the need to maintain a positive attitude towards science, he asserts, "I am a nuclear physicist by training and a deeply committed Christian." He believes that God created the entire universe. But, he does not take everything written in the Bible literally. He acknowledges the role of science in unfolding the mystery of God. "We are exploring space and sub-atomic particles and learning new facts every day, facts that the creator has known since the beginning of time," he said.

Carter also says parts of the Bible were based on outdated social structures and that "the basic principles of the Bible are taught by God, but, written down by human beings deprived of modern day knowledge" (Raushenbush 2012).

Based on the Bible, he believes in the basic equality among humans: "I believe what Paul taught in Galatians that there is no distinction in God's eyes between men and women, slaves and masters, Jews and non-Jews – everybody is created equally in the eyes of God" (Gal 3:28).

This makes him open to and respectful of homosexuals. "Homosexuality was well known in the ancient world, much before Christ was born and Jesus never said a word about homosexuality. In all of his teachings about multiple things, he never said that gay people should be condemned. I personally think, it is very fine for gay people to be married in civil ceremonies."

He urges his readers "to emulate what Christ did as he faced people who were despised like the lepers". Christ reached out to poor people and those who were different and treated them equally. "The more despised and the more in need they were, the more he emphasised that we should go to and share with them our talent our ability, our wealth, our influence" (Raushenbush 2012).

> There are many verses in the Bible that you could interpret very rigidly and that makes you ultimately a fundamentalist. When you think you are better than anybody else, that you are closer to God than other people, and, therefore, they are inferior to you and subhuman – that leads to conflict and hatred and dissonance among people when we should be working for peace.

He pleads with the Christians to be respectful of other faiths. "Jesus also taught that we should not judge other people and that it is God who judges people." So, we should not be judging other religious traditions too. Such an attitude helps him to be committed to his own faith and at the same time to be open to other faith traditions.

"There are many verses in the Bible that you could interpret very rigidly and that makes you ultimately a fundamentalist. When you think you are better than anybody else, that you are closer to God than other people, and, therefore, they are inferior to you and subhuman – that leads to conflict and hatred and dissonance among people when we should be working for peace."

The greatness of this political leader is that his life is based on his religious conviction, but without clinging on slavishly to them.

69

The God in the God Particle is All Around

Scientists at the world's biggest atom smasher, CERN, in Geneva, announced that they have gathered enough evidence to show that the long-sought after "God particle", answering fundamental questions about the universe, almost certainly does exist.

The researchers at CERN's vast complex on the Swiss-French border says the massive data they have obtained will essentially show the footprint of the key particle known as the Higgs boson. CERN's atom smasher, the $10-billion Large Hadron Collider (LHC), has been creating high-energy collisions of protons to help them understand suspected phenomena, such as dark matter, antimatter and ultimately the creation of the universe 13 billion years ago, which scientists believe occurred as a massive explosion, known as the Big Bang.

On 4 July, the two main experiments at the LHC (ATLAS and CMS) both reported independently the confirmed existence of a previously unknown particle with a mass of about 133 proton masses that is "consistent with the Higgs boson" and widely believed to be the God particle (AP 2012).

The discovery of the Higgs boson, also named after Satyendra Nath Bose, will not change people's lives, but will help explain the underpinnings of the universe. It would confirm the standard model of physics that explains why fundamental particles have mass. Those particles are the building blocks of the universe. Mass is a trait that combines with gravity to give an object weight.

The phrase God particle, coined by Nobel Prize-winning physicist Leon Lederman, is used by laymen, not physicists, more as an explanation for how the wonders of the subatomic universe work than how it all started. The original intended name, was actually, 'Goddamn particle'.

For a genuine believer, anything that advances human knowledge also advances human wisdom. Any human ach¬ievement, including scientific ones, is a sign of God being present among us.

Though an impenetrable concept to many, the Higgs boson has until now been just that a concept intended to explain a riddle: How subatomic particles, such as electrons and protons, had mass (AP 2012). The answer came in a theory first proposed by physicist Peter Higgs and others in 1964. It envisioned an energy field where particles interact with a key particle, the Higgs boson.

The idea is that other particles attract Higgs boson and the more they attract, the bigger their mass will be. Some liken the effect to a ubiquitous Higgs snowfield that affects other particles travelling through it, depending on whether they are wearing, metaphorically speaking, snowshoes or just shoes.

As a religious believer, when we discover a great scientific theory, it is surely something we can be proud of. This discovery shows that in our ongoing search for the fundamental nature of matter, we are moving in the right direction. So, we can truly congratulate the scientists and wish them further success.

For a genuine believer, anything that advances human knowledge also advances human wisdom. Any human achievement, including scientific ones, is a sign of God being present among us. Therefore, it is good to wonder at God particle and marvel at the ingenuity of our scientific age. At the same time, we should not be blind to the fact that God, if it is God, is present everywhere. The old fashioned atoms and the obsolete ether also reflect God in their own ways. So to limit the presence and activity of God to God particle is a mistake. The extraordinary discoveries like God particle should make us pause and look at the grandeur of reality, including our own inner consciousness.

70

Altruism Opens All of Us to the Divine

In a recent scientific study, it was found that the part of the brain we use when engaging in egalitarian behaviour may also be linked to altruism and our relationship to the larger environment. The study conducted by researchers from the five prestigious North American universities is based on the previous findings which established that two areas of the brain, including the insular cortex, are active when we behave in an egalitarian manner. These areas are connected to the sense of altruism, reciprocity, fairness and aversion to inequality.

To explore further, the egalitarian behaviour in a group setting, the researchers conducted an experiment in which individuals played a game to study the brain activity in the process of decision-making. As reported recently in *Science Daily* (New York University 2012), in the 'random income game' participants in a group are randomly assigned a level of income and the group is assigned to one of the three income distributions. Subjects are shown the income of all members of their group, including their own, on a computer screen. Individuals are then asked if they wish to pay a cost in order to increase or decrease the incomes of group members. Subjects are told they need not give away the money to the others shown on their screen. Therefore, there is a strong incentive not to part with any of the money already allocated to them. Nonetheless, the study found that the participants frequently sought to reallocate resources so the money was more equally distributed among the group members.

During this period, the researchers gauged the subjects' neurological activity through functional magnetic resonance

Adam Smith maintained that moral sentiments like egalitarianism was derived from a 'fellow feeling' that would increase with our level of sympathy for others.

imaging. As shown in previous studies, the researchers found significant activity in the brain's insular cortex.

But, to get at a more detailed understanding of neurological activity during these behaviours, they also studied whether activations in these areas were associated with two additional measures of egalitarian preferences. As part of a survey, subjects were asked about their level of agreement or disagreement to six questions, which included: "Our society should do whatever is necessary to make sure that everyone has an equal opportunity to succeed", and, "This country would be better off if we worried less about how equal people are" (New York University 2012). In addition, subjects completed a series of decision-making tasks asking them to split money with another anonymous person. The choices individuals make here are a measure of egalitarian behaviour.

The researchers found that these two measures of egalitarian preferences were significantly associated with activations in the insular cortex.

This particular result is potentially a very significant one because the insular cortex is also the part of the brain that processes the relationship of the individual with respect to the environment. In other words, from a neurological perspective, egalitarian behaviour may not exist in isolation, but is part of a larger process that stems from altruism and a sense of the larger social good.

Already, in the 18th century Adam Smith maintained that moral sentiments like egalitarianism was derived from a 'fellow feeling' that would increase with our level of sympathy for others. Our brain, including our consciousness, may be evolving to encompass the larger reality that confronts us today. It may be that in this very process of opening ourselves to the larger world, with fairness, altruism and egalitarianism, we experience the divine in ourselves and in the other. For compassion necessarily helps us reach God.

71

Language and God

We assume that language is to communicate our thoughts about the world. Recent studies have shown that language is an essential aspect of ourselves and of the world. Long ago, the Roman emperor Charlemagne observed: "*To speak another language is to possess another soul.*" The language we use gives us a sense of self and of identity. Our personality and self-understanding is shaped by the language we use.

Some Harvard psychologists found that bilingual individuals' opinions of different ethnic groups were affected by the language in which they took a test examining their biases and predilections. In other words, they concluded that our language may influence not only our thoughts, but our implicit preferences as well.

The result of this study appearing in *The Journal of Experimental Social Psychology* is quoted by *Daily Science* (Harvard University 2010). Oludamini Ogunnaike, one of the authors says: "This study suggests that language is much more than a medium for expressing thoughts and feelings. Our work hints that language creates and shapes our thoughts and feelings as well" (Harvard University 2010).Implicit attitudes and positive or negative associations tend to shape the behavior towards members of social groups. The above experiment has shown that these attitudes depend on factors such as the language we speak.

"Can we shift something as fundamental as what we like and dislike by changing the language in which our preferences are elicited?"

> Definitely language does not merely express but adds to our experience of the divine. May be the Indian seers had instinctually perceived the power of language in experiencing God when they evoked the power of mantras.

co-author Mahzarin R. Banaji asks. His answer is affirmative. Employing Implicit Association Test (IAT), the researchers asked the participants to categorize words rapidly and unreflectively that flash on a computer screen are played through headphones. "The IAT bypasses a large part of conscious cognition and taps into something we're not aware of and can't easily control," Banaji notes.

The researchers administered the IAT in two different settings: once in Morocco, with bilinguals in Arabic and French, and again in the U.S. with people who speak both English and Spanish. In Morocco, participants showed greater preference for other Moroccans. When they took the test in French, that difference disappeared. Similarly, in the U.S., participants who took the test in Spanish showed a greater preference for other Hispanics. But again, in English, that preference disappeared.

"It was quite shocking to see that a person could take the same test, within a brief period of time, and show such different results." Ogunnaike elaborates. "It's like asking your friend if he likes ice cream in English, and then turning around and asking him again in French and getting a different answer" (Harvard University 2010).

It was the eminent linguist Benjamin Lee Whorf who proposed in the 1930s that language is so powerful that it can even determine thought. He asserted: "Language shapes the way we think, and determines what we can think about." Mainstream psychology has taken a rather sceptical view that while language may affect thought processes, it doesn't influence thought itself. This new study tends to agree that language, in fact, determines thought and shapes our tastes.

"These results challenge our views of attitudes as stable," Banaji says. "There still remain some bigger questions about just how fixed or flexible they are, and language may provide a window through which we will learn about their nature."

Such scientific insights pose significant questions for religious language and experience. If our attitudes are shaped by the language we employ, surely our attitude about and even experience of God is also conditioned by our language. Definitely language does not merely express but adds to our experience of the divine. May be the Indian seers had instinctually perceived the power of language in experiencing God when they evoked the power of mantras.

Lessons from Life

72

We See What We Want to, and Need to See

If you are looking for a particular object, say a yellow pencil, on a crowded desk, how does your brain work to visually locate it? For the first time, neuroscientists identified how the brain works to select what we want to see. A team led by Carnegie Mellon University neuroscientists has identified how different neural regions communicate to determine what to pay attention to and what to ignore.

The study, reported in *Science Daily*, used various brain-imaging techniques to show exactly how the visual cortex and parietal cortex send direct information to each other through white matter connections in order to specifically pick out the information that you want to see (Carnegie Mellon University 2012).

Adam S. Greenberg, the lead author of the study, said, "We have demonstrated that attention is a process in which there is one-to-one mapping between the first-place visual information coming from the eyes into the brain and beyond to other parts of the brain."

It is incredible how an entire system is working in the background to accomplish a simple task. "With so much information in the visual world, it's dramatic to think that you have an entire system behind knowing what to pay attention to," said Marlene Behrmann, a professor of psychology. She adds, "The mechanisms show that you can actually drive the visual system – you are guiding your own sensory system in an intelligent and smart fashion that helps facilitate your actions in the world."

As part of the study, the research team conducted two sets of experiments with five adults. They first used several different functional brain scans to identify regions in the brain responsible for visual processing and attention. In one experiment, the participants had to look at a dot in the centre of the screen while six stimuli danced around the dot and distracted them. The second task encouraged the participants to respond to the stimuli one at a time. These scans determined the regions in both the visual and parietal cortices. The researchers could then look for connectivity between these regions and study the areas of the brain connected to paying full attention and partial attention.

The second part of the experiment collected anatomical data of the brain's white matter while the participants had their brains scanned without performing any tasks. Then, the researchers combined the results with those from the functional experiments to show how white matter is significant in paying full attention and partial attention. The results showed that white matter connections are mapped systematically. This implies that there are direct connections between corresponding visual field locations in the visual cortex and the parietal cortex.

Thus, different regions of the brain interact together to focus on what we want to do. They work together while paying special attention to one specific aspect or ignoring other aspects. So the success of human attention or concentration is dependent on our ability to filter our irrelevant information. "Because we know that training can alter white matter, it might be possible, through training, that the ability to filter out irrelevant or unwanted information could be improved," Greenberg said (Carnegie Mellon University 2012).

In general, we know that "selective perception" is part of a human way of dealing with the world outside. Thus, the study has shown that different parts of the brain work together to enable us to see what we want to see and what we need to see, at the cost of apparent useless or irrelevant information.

73

Moving through Birth and Death

It is insightful to watch the flow and direction of a flock of birds. If we imagine anything moving as a swarm – animals, birds, bacteria, molecules within cells, cancer cells, fish, and even tiny plastic rods on a vibrating table – we wonder what really guides them. Who gives them a sense of direction? And how?

According to theoretical physicist John J. Toner of the University of Oregon, US, they just keep on moving, unhindered even by deaths and births.

In an article published in the February 24, 2012 in the journal *Physical Review Letters*, the scientist shows that flocking persists and can withstand even individual birth and death. The finding, he said, "is especially important for many other organisms that flock, especially bacteria, which may contain millions of individuals that are constantly dying and being replaced by the reproduction of others as the swarm moves" (University of Oregon 2012).

Taken collectively, humanity moves forward and is independent of each one of us, although, at times, we may influence the direction of humanity decisively.

He elaborates: "A flock can keep moving in the same direction for times much longer than the lifetime of any individual member. Individuals are being born and dying, but, their direction and motion can persist much longer than the lifetime of any individual creature" (University of Oregon 2012).

He admitted that the changes in the number of such "mortal flock"– where some members are leaving by death and joining by birth – can create "persistent but predictable fluctuations". But, they do not significantly alter the direction of the flow. This is applicable both to living beings and to non-living flow.

Studying the movement of molecules within cells, Toner spoke of individual molecules living only for about 20 minutes, but, collectively these cells live and continue their work for days. Toner asserts: "The motion continues as dead molecules are replaced by newly synthesised molecules, as well as by molecules that immigrate in to take their places."

As reported in *Science Daily*, this study has implications in biology, and, eventually, could point to new cancer therapies. Further, "This study shows us how fundamental physics and mathematics deployed to explain an everyday occurrence in nature can spin off with potentially life-saving medical applications," said Kimberly Andrews Espy, vice-president for research and innovation at the University of Oregon.

It is truly insightful to apply the lessons of swarm to humanity as a whole. Taken collectively, humanity moves forward and is independent of each one of us, although, at times, we may influence the direction of humanity decisively.

Traditional religions console us saying that the human destiny or movement is guided, directed and led by God. In his hands, religions tell us, humanity can rest at ease, in spite of some turbulence that we experience in our daily life. Agnostics and atheists may not have a clear understanding of the flow of life, but, they can very well talk of the "vital force" that sustains everyone.

Be that as it may, our individual life does make sense only within the larger framework of our collective movement. Our individual destiny, even in its failure, is irrevocably linked to the collective and unconscious movement of the whole, towards which we may, even against our will, contribute something. Thus, the great marvel of my individual life – with its own progress, regress and development – is that I am somehow part of a larger flow of humanity. Is it guided by someone or self-propelling? Although, we do not know the answer to this perplexing question, we do know that our individual destiny is intrinsically tied to our collective destiny. That's indeed marvellous!

74

Lessons from Junk Food

Recently, it was experimentally proved that junk food can cause rats to become so addicted to it that they will starve themselves rather than eat healthy food. Published in the journal *Nature Neuroscience*, two scientists Paul Johnson and Paul Kenny have shown that rats' response to unlimited junk food closely parallels well-known patterns of drug addiction (Johnson & Kenny 2010).

In their study, they fed rats on either a balanced diet or on unlimited access to junk foods. Within a short time period, the rats on the junk food diet began to eat compulsively and quickly became overweight. "They're taking in twice the amount of calories as the control rats," Kenny observed.

The researchers hypothesized that the rats were eating compulsively because, like drug addicts, they had become desensitized to smaller amounts and needed more and more for the same amount of pleasure. Usually drugs work by directly stimulating the brain's pleasure centers, particularly the dopamine receptor known as D2. Overstimulation of this receptor causes the body to start producing less dopamine, leading the addict to compensate by taking more of the drug. Dopamine can also be released by healthy activities such as food, exercise or sex.

Kenny and Johnson showed that desensitization of the receptors occurred after just five days on a junk food diet. "They're not experiencing rewards the way they should," Kenny added. "When you experience that, one way of feeling better is to go back to the junk food." In other words: "They lose control. This is the hallmark of addiction" (Scripps Research Institute 2010).

> True spirituality is not running away from the world, but it is being immersed in the world and reaching out to this world, without being enamoured by its glamour. True spirituality is to relish the normal food!

In another test the scientists used a virus to block the D2 receptors in healthy rats. Immediately afterwards, they become compulsive eaters. "This is the most complete evidence to date that suggests obesity and drug addiction have common neurobiological underpinnings," Johnson claimed.

Having established that the junk food rats had become addicted, Johnson and Kenny wanted to know how far this addiction would push them. So they took both junk-food addicted rats and ordinary rats and exposed them to electrical shocks whenever they ate junk. Rats that had just been introduced to junk food quickly stopped eating it, while the addicted rats ignored the discomfort and kept eating.

The most shocking finding came when they removed the addicted rats' access to junk food and started feeding them only healthy food again -- the same diets the rats had eaten earlier. When junk food was no longer available, the rats simply refused to eat for two weeks. "They actually voluntarily starved themselves," Kenny said. "It's almost as if you break these things, it's very, very hard to go back to the way things were before. Their dietary preferences are dramatically shifted" (Scripps Research Institute 2010).

To a limited extent, moderate amount of junk food may serve as a function. But when we get addicted to them, they dominate and mould us. The same is true of spirituality. To some extent, we need healthy distractions and even illusions. Delusions, at times, may have even functional value. For example, if an delusion can free an addict of his smoking, it has functional, not absolute, value.

So healthy spirituality urges us to realize our illusions, distractions and even the need for them. It makes us careful not to get addicted to them. Healthy spirituality knows how far we can tolerate junk thoughts, wasted energy and meaningless illusions. It knows the relative role of *maya* in our lives and at the same time is careful not to get immersed in it, not to be absorbed in it, not to be overwhelmed by it. Thus true spirituality is not running away from the world, but it is being immersed in the world and reaching out to this world, without being enamoured by its glamour. True spirituality is to relish the normal food!

75

Grief is a Universal Experience for All

Religion comes to our aid, especially when we grieve the demise of a beloved. Contemporary world atheists face an added dilemma in grieving the loss of their own beloved.

A few years ago, when Rebecca Hensler, a 43-year-old school counsellor from America, lost her infant son, she received numerous condolence messages. Although, their intentions were good, but their words weren't always so good. And in the rawness of her grief, Hensler found some of them downright hurtful. She felt hurt and humiliated to be told that her three-month-old son is "an angel, or part of God's plan, or in a better place than in his mother's arms".

Hensler spoke at monthly gathering of non-theists. "(Atheists) don't think we are going to get to hold our children again," she said. "We are facing an absolute loss, so when someone projects onto that the idea that we are going to be able to hold our children again or communicate with them, it is essentially dismissing the magnitude of that loss" (Winston 2012).

As the atheist community grows and becomes established, people are looking for a way to process grief and sorrow without the support of religious ritual, belief and structures. So she founded "Grief Beyond Belief", a Facebook page where non-believers can share their grief in what she describes as "a safe place" without God-talk.

Hensler posts something new every day – a link, a picture, a question, a thought. Some of the recent topics include a discussion of travel as a balm for pain, a look at how agnostics grieve, and a link to a "Bill of Rights for the Grieving". Right number seven in this Bill is: "You have the right not to be grateful, reasonable, inspired or inspiring."

The idea that non-believers need their own places to grieve is gaining ground in atheist circles. The book Godless Grief, written by Cathe Jones, which was published in 2009, attempted to answer this need. Atheist Nexus, an online community of non-theists, established a grief support group last year; and in recent months, some serious atheist bloggers have taken up the topic, as Kimberly Winston of Religious News Service points out in *The Huffington Post.*

Rabbi Peter Schweitzer, leader of New York's The City Congregation for Humanistic Judaism, which has long held secular funeral services, holds that grief is a universal experience that requires different responses. He says, "Secular people feel as racked with sorrow as the next person." Then he adds, "Christians mourn differently than Jews who mourn differently than Muslims. There ought to be space for those who don't share religious beliefs to mourn, too" (Winston 2012).

For convinced atheists, John Lennon's famous song, "Imagine there's no heaven," isn't just a lyric, but reality. And it's not always easy but the struggle is worth it.

Whether we are atheists or believers, we need to grieve for the tragedies of our life. A caring and compassionate community support is essential for such grieving. Some kind of structure helps such a grieving process. Even without cheap consolation and theoretical foundations, human beings necessarily need community and structures to cope with such ambiguities of our daily life. If religion, with God, helps in grieving and, thus, coping with life, that is fine. If atheism, without God, enables us to grieve and thus cope with life, it has to be appreciated. In both cases, let us truly confront the tragedy, grieve adequately and learn to move on compassionately!

76

The Missing Gene

Latest scientific research suggests that in fact, losing 510 chunks of DNA may have enabled humans to develop bigger brains, spineless penises and other human traits as reported in the Journal *Nature,* March 2011. The research is the latest attempt to find genetic factors that make humans unique. Previously researchers have searched for genes that humans have but other species do not, but the new study looks for missing human genetic material during the course of evolution.

Stanford researchers David Kingsley and Gill Bejerano looked for missing DNA that could shape human uniqueness. The team looked at the genetic blueprints of humans, chimpanzees and macaques to see if humans were missing genetic material. They found that humans "lack many chunks of DNA that chimps, macaques and mice all seem to share – at least 510 different bits, sometime between 500,000 and 6 million years ago" (Howard Hughes Medical Institute 2011).

Only one of the missing bits contained an actual gene. The rest of the absent genetic instructions may be important switches for turning on genes. Such switches, also called enhancers, may be located far from a gene but still govern when and where the gene is flipped on during development.

It is known that humans and chimps have roughly the same set of genes, and yet have clear physical and behavioral differences. Some scientists think that changing the way genes are used – by turning a

> Both presence and absence shape us, differently and distinctly. The missing part may be quite significant in our precious lives. The dynamic play between shadow and light, life and death may really deepen collectively inter-connected consciousness.

gene on or off in a particular tissue or during a phase of development – may be a way to evolve new characteristics without damaging important genes. Adding or deleting enhancers is one way to regulate gene activity.

Because most of the missing chunks of DNA don't contain genes, it is difficult to say exactly what the pieces are supposed to do. The scientists used "a very clever computational analysis" to figure out the functioning of this chunk, as reported in *ScienceNews* (Saey 2011).

The researchers found that one piece of DNA missing in humans is an enhancer for the gene, which controls the production of facial sensory whiskers and small spines on the penises of both chimps and mice, the researchers found. Since humans don't have this enhancer, the particular gene is not turned on, and so sensory whiskers and penile spines fail to develop.

In many mammals, penile spines are prominent, help males achieve ejaculation quickly. "The key to reproductive success is impregnation, and the faster you can achieve that, the better," says Owen Lovejoy, a biological anthropologist. But even though the loss of the spines makes copulation last longer, it hasn't hurt the reproductive success of humans. "Longer copulation times may help cement bonds between mating partners" asserts Lovejoy. Such bonds have been "a key to humans' evolutionary success" (Saey 2011).

Another missing enhancer explains the evolution of human brain size. The enhancer lies next to a tumor-suppressing gene, which normally controls cell growth so that cancer doesn't develop. In mice and chimps, the enhancer DNA turns the gene on in the brain. Since humans lack this enhancer, the gene is not turned on in the brain and brain cells may proliferate, possibly contributing to bigger brains.

These are some of the factors that contribute to the uniqueness of human beings. But it is interesting that partly these specificities are brought about by the absence of genetic enhancers. So we owe so much of our uniqueness to the absence of genetic stuff, as to their presence.

This speaks a lot about our own lives. Both presence and absence shape us, differently and distinctly. The missing part may be quite significant in our precious lives. The dynamic play between shadow and light, life and death may really deepen collectively interconnected consciousness.

77

Egocentricity Subverts Efforts to Know Others

Spiritual vision enables us to perceive things clearly and to be in touch with our true selves, going beyond our inauthentic egos. The famous Indian philosopher and educationalist Mrinal Miri talks of the need to overcome "egocentricity" to become spiritual.

According to Miri, egocentricity "distorts, to a greater or less extent, most of our perceptions of reality, and this is especially true of our perception of human reality". Egocentricity also subverts our efforts to know another person and, thus, we need to overcome it. Such an overcoming of our ego in opening ourselves to another person is never an isolated phenomenon, but a common project, leading to genuine humility. Miri elaborates: "To be able to transcend one's ego is also to be able to achieve true humility; and with humility comes the realisation of the infinite difficulty of being just to another person. The realisation, in other words, of the ever-present possibility that one has blotted out, from one's attention, vital, if not subtle, aspects of the other person's behaviour."

Overcoming egocentricity and opening up to the other person leads us to ahimsa. So he adds: "A natural accompaniment of such a realisation on the way to achieving the true emotion of love, or what Gandhi, M." might have meant by ahimsa. And it is the possibility of ahimsa in this sense that makes knowledge of the other as a person possible."

Commenting on these insights, professor Ananta Kumar Giri, faculty of the Madras Institute of Development Studies, sees the connection between overcoming of ego and fostering genuine relationships with others. According to Giri, "Overcoming egocentricity helps one realise humility and ahimsa in one's knowledge of and relationship with the other."

> We have to recognise that ordinarily, violence is rooted in dogmatic and mistaken knowledge claim that fail to recognise other legitimate perspectives. Thus, Anekantavada provides us with an alternative lifestyle to support dialogue among people of diverse viewpoints.

This process of fostering humility and ahimsa is facilitated by a proper and an adequate understanding of *Anekantavada*, one of the fundamental doctrines of Jainism. According to this theory, the notion that truth and reality are perceived differently from diverse points of view. Emphasising pluralism or multiplicity of viewpoints, it affirms that no single point of view possesses the complete truth.

According to Giri, there are three tenets of *Anekantavada*. The first one is that there is a possibility of many perceptions of an object. The second tenet affirms that everything is relative and multi-dimensional. The third tenet is that there is an in-built coexistence of opposites, that one dimension is possible as another and it is only in relation to other factors like time, place and context that one dimension gains predominance over another. All this is subsumed under the doctrine of *Syadavada*. It may be best described as: "(1) May be, it is; (2) may be, it is not; (3) may be, it is and it is not; (4) may be, it is indescribable; (5) may be, it is and yet is indescribable; (6) may be, it is not and it is also indescribable; and (7) may be, it is and it is not and it is also indescribable."

It is by accepting such multi-dimensional nature of objects and their probability that we can derive the moral imperative overcoming egocentricity leading to ahimsa. Giri points out that historically, *Anekantavada* was directly related to Mahavira's philosophy of ahimsa. We have to recognise that ordinarily, violence is rooted in dogmatic and mistaken knowledge claim that fail to recognise other legitimate perspectives. Thus, *Anekantavada* provides us with an alternative lifestyle to support dialogue among people of diverse viewpoints.

78

The Imperative of Fostering Life

Recently there was a scientific study which concludes that "having an abortion does not increase the risk of mental health problems, but having a baby does."

The research conducted by Danish scientists claims to debunk the notion that terminating a pregnancy can trigger mental illness. It further indicates that the postpartum depression can be a serious factor. The research was published in *New England Journal of Medicine*, and was reported in *The Huffington Post* (Chang 2011).

The study included 365,550 teenagers and women who had an abortion or first-time delivery between 1995 and 2007. The study included only those who did not have a history of psychiatric problems that needed hospitalization. During the study period, 84,620 had an abortion while 280,930 participants gave birth. Through various sources, researchers were able to track mental health counseling at a hospital or outpatient facility before and after an abortion or delivery.

Researchers compared the rate of mental health treatment among women before and after a first abortion. Within the first year after an abortion, 15 per 1,000 women needed psychiatric counseling – similar to the rate seeking help nine months before an abortion. In fact researchers assumed women who seek abortions hail from a demographic group which is more likely to have emotional problems to begin with."

Protection and fostering of life is the most sacred duty and is an unassailable imperative. Here we have no choice, whatever be the price we have to pay.

While first-time mothers had an overall lower rate of mental problems overall, the proportion of those seeking help after giving birth was dramatically higher. About 7 per 1,000 women got mental health help within a year of giving birth compared with 4 per 1,000 women before the delivery of the child.

The most common problems among women in both the abortion and the delivery groups were debilitating anxiety, severe stress and depression. After an abortion, "a woman should know that her risk of having a psychiatric episode is not increased" said Trine Munk-Olsen of Aarhus University, the leader of the study (Chang 2011).

The study did not examine why a pregnancy was terminated. Researchers studied only the mental problems serious enough to warrant admission to a hospital or outpatient clinic and did not look into the role of mild depression and other lesser symptoms.

In a previous study, published in 2006, Munk-Olsen found new mothers faced increased risks for a host of mental problems, not just postpartum depression. Changes in hormone levels, sleep deprivation and other demands associated with having a baby could trigger mental problems, experts say. By contrast, women who have an abortion don't experience similar changes. "Anyone who's ever had a baby knows it's stressful. That stress doesn't go away in a week or two" after delivery, said Dr. Robert Blum, who specializes in this area.

The latest findings, the authors claim, echo an extensive review by the *American Psychological Association* in 2008 that found no evidence that ending an unwanted pregnancy threatens women's mental health.

A separate review by Blum and his colleagues found that "the most rigorous research on the topic did not find a relationship between abortion and long-term mental health problems" (Chang 2011).

To claim that bringing a baby into the world is more mentally stressful that terminating it before it is born, is saying too much. Such a claim cannot be accepted by any civilized society. My basic response to such a claim is that what is assumed as mental health can very well be maintained by the worst of offenders, particularly if the offender loses all sense of shame and guilt which normally occur after repeated. On the other hand, when it comes to promoting life, the most sacred asset of ours, no amount of tension can stand on our way. Protection and fostering of life is the most sacred duty and is an unassailable imperative. Here, we have no choice, whatever be the price we have to pay.

79

Extending Care and Compassion

Early humans like Neanderthals had developed a deep seated sense of compassion that belied their primitive reputation, according to Jennifer Viegas, from *Discovery News* (University of York 2010). Referring to a research conducted by the University of York, England, there is evidence indicating that around 500,000 and 40,000 years ago, early humans like the Neanderthals, developed concern and commitment to others.

The study concluded from archeological findings that injured or sick members of their group were routinely cared for. Remains examined by the scholars revealed a child with a congenital brain abnormality was not abandoned, but cared for until five or six years old. In another case a Neanderthal with a withered arm, deformed feet and blindness in one eye was attended to for about 20 years.

The interdependence of early communities, who would hunt and eat together, let to an emerging commitment to the welfare of each other. Based on fossils and artifacts, the scientists propose a four stage model for the development of human compassion:

The first stage began six million years ago when the common ancestor of humans and chimpanzees experienced the initial awakenings of an empathy for others and motivation to help them, perhaps "with a gesture of comfort, or moving a branch to allow them to pass."

The second stage from 1.8 million years ago sees compassion in *Homo erectus* as an evolving emotion integrated with rational thought. Care of sick individuals represented an extensive compassionate investment while the special treatment of the dead suggested grief at the loss of a loved one and a desire to soothe others feelings, the researchers say (University of York 2010).

The third stage, based on findings between around 500,000 and 40,000 years ago, sees Neanderthals developing deep-seated commitments to the welfare of others necessitated by a long childhood and adolescence and a dependence on hunting together. There is also archaeological evidence of the routine care of the injured or infirm over extended periods.

In **the fourth stage**, the scientists say modern humans starting 120,000 years ago extended compassion to strangers, animals, objects and abstract concepts. We are still at this stage now.

The research, published in the journal *Time and Mind*, indicated that concern and compassion were demonstrated through care of sick individuals, representing an extensive compassionate investment. Particularly the emergence of special treatment of the dead suggested "grief at the loss of a loved one and a desire to soothe others' feelings," the scholars concluded. Dr Penny Spikins, who headed the study, maintained that new research developments, such as neuro-imaging, have enabled archaeologists to attempt a scientific explanation of what was "once intangible feelings of ancient humans". She added: "Compassion is perhaps the most fundamental human emotion. It binds us together and can inspire us but it is also fragile and elusive" (University of York 2010).

> May be it is by investing in this "fragile and elusive" project of extending our compassion to the whole life, that we humans can experience our own uniqueness!

"This apparent fragility makes addressing the evidence for the development of compassion in our most ancient ancestors a unique challenge, yet the archaeological record has an important story to tell about the prehistory of compassion." She added: "We have traditionally paid a lot of attention to how early humans thought about each other, but it may well be time to pay rather more attention to whether or not they 'cared'."

The question confronting us moderns is: Can we foster further such a "fragile and elusive" compassion which evolved in the course of human evolution? May be it is in furthering such a compassion that we attain our moral and spiritual maturity! May be it is by investing in this "fragile and elusive" project of extending our compassion to the whole life, that we humans can experience our own uniqueness!

80

Italy, India, Indonesia

The movie "Eat, Love, Pray" which stars American actress Julia Roberts released on Friday, August 13, 2010 raises some spiritual questions. The movie is based on a 2006 memoir by American author Elizabeth Gilbert, "Eat, Pray, Love: One Woman's Search for Everything Across Italy, India and Indonesia," which was in the *New York Times* Best Seller list for more than 158 weeks (Gilbert 2010). It echoes the author's experience and spiritual discoveries in these three countries.

At the age of 32, Elizabeth Gilbert was educated, had a home and a husband, and a successful career as a writer. However, she was unhappy in her marriage and often spent nights crying in her bathroom. So, she takes the initiative for a divorce, which her husband contested. The actual process of divorce leaves lonely. So she goes for a one year tour to all three countries. The main reason she decides to take her trip is that she knows she deserves happiness and a joy in life, which she felt she no longer had. Briefly, she goes to Italy to eat, to pray in India and to discover love in Bali.

She spent four months in Italy, eating and enjoying herself physically. In Italy, a fellow gives a long speech about how Americans look for entertainment but don't understand the simple pleasures of life. She is told that the American life style of rushing through their meals and rushing around is not healthy. Further, she learned about the sweetness of doing nothing in Italy.

Then she spent four months in India, finding her spirituality. In the movie, Julie Roberts does service in India by scrubbing the floors of the temple to experience spiritual insights (Smock 2013). Here she learns to meditate and forgive herself for the divorce she has initiated.

She spent the year in Bali, Indonesia. At that time an old man from Bali tells her that she must find a balance in her life. When one learns to balance herself and her life to be healthy from inside and out. While looking for "balance" of the two she discovers love in the form of a dashing Brazilian factory owner.

Maureen Callahan of the *New York Post* dislikes the book for its simplistic focus on Eastern religion. She heavily criticized the book, calling it "narcissistic New Age reading," and "the worst in Western fetishization of Eastern thought and culture, assured in its answers to existential dilemmas that have confounded intellects greater than hers." Further, she was highly critical of her fans who are "indulging in this silliness" (Smock 2013).

The book and the movie have great many admirers. In fact Ashrams are set up and tours are organised based on the Eat, Pray and Love principle. But we need to remind ourselves that the book as well as the novel is not about a human being's travel to exotic locations for a year to make herself feel better and happier. The story is more about self discovery, the search for happiness and understanding what it is to love and to be loved unconditionally.

Though the book and the movie tend to give some naive answers we can still learn the simple insight that there is so much of emptiness in our contemporary culture: for food, spirituality and love. That just cannot be answered by change of location, but change of heart. The three locations can very well be seen as symbols of -the human need for physical, emotional and spiritual well-being, which can only be attained by sustained commitment and rigorous practice.

More fundamental to the issue is: When one seeks spirituality and balance, do we need to presuppose a reality, usually God or Transcendence, all powerful, all-embracing and all-loving: the source and destiny of ourselves?

81

Plants Recognise Kin and Act Altruistically

The concept of altruism has long been debated in philosophical and religious circles, and more recently, scientists and evolutionary biologists have taken up this issue. From the perspective of natural selection, altruism may have evolved because any action that improves the likelihood of a relative's survival and reproduction increases the chance of an individual's DNA being passed on.

Social behaviour, kin recognition, and altruism are well known in the animal kingdom, not among plants. Though plants have the ability to respond to other plants, their ability to recognise kin and act altruistically has been the subject of recent studies. In a paper published in November, Guillermo Murphy and Susan Dudley explore kin recognition in yellow jewelweed (American Journal of Botany 2009). Yellow jewelweed individuals are often found growing in close proximity to related individuals and are known to respond strongly to aboveground competition, making this species a likely candidate for kin recognition.

Murphy and Dudley measured plants' responses to two potential cues for competition – changes in light quality (an aboveground cue) and the presence of root neighbours (an underground cue) – for plants grown with strangers and with relatives. The researchers found that the response of the other plants differed depending on whether the plants grew with relatives or with strangers. This demonstrates that jewelweed is capable of recognizing kin from non-kin. It further

As socially connected beings, our spiritual challenge is to live truly as members of *Vasudeva kudumbakam*. If we fail, we are failing our duty to life – in its diversity and richness – itself.

indicates an interesting degree of complexity since both types of responses differed from plants growing with no neighbours at all. If living among close relatives, plants did not increase resource allocation to roots or leaves. Rather, they altered their aboveground morphology by increasing stem elongation and branching (American Journal of Botany 2009). These plants are cooperating with kin by attempting to acquire needed resources without shading nearby relatives. Yellow jewelweed is found in the under story of forests, where light may be scarce but the soil is usually nutrient-rich. Because light is the limiting factor for plant growth in this environment, a plant competing with its neighbours would be most likely to allocate resources to leaves.

These plants, when grown with strangers, increased their resource allocation to their leaves relative to allocation to stems and roots, an indication of a competitive response. By moving their resources into leaves, these plants not only positively affected their own growth by enhancing their ability to acquire a limited resource but also negatively affected their competitors' growth by shading nearby plants and decreasing the competitor's light acquisition abilities. Scientists hold that communication among roots may be necessary for plants to recognise kin. In a different research, Susan Dudley, found that when plants share their pots, they get competitive and start growing more roots, which allows them to grab water and mineral nutrients before their neighbours get them. "It appears, though, that they only do this when sharing a pot with unrelated plants. Because differences between groups of strangers and groups of siblings only occurred when they shared a pot, the root interactions may provide a cue for kin recognition."

This study demonstrates that plants are social organisms, just like animals and human beings. As socially connected beings, our spiritual challenge is to live truly as members of *Vasudeva kudumbakam*. If we fail, we are failing our duty to life – in its diversity and richness – itself.

Bibliography

American Friends of Tel Aviv University (July 29, 2010). Can't place that face?. *Science Daily*. Retrieved December 15, 2013, from http://www.*ScienceDaily*.com/releases/2010/07/100728151429.htm

American Journal of Botany (2009, November 12). Can a plant be altruistic?. *Science Daily*. Retrieved December 21, 2013, from http://www.*ScienceDaily*.com/releases/2009/11/091111092047.htm

AP. (2012, July 2). Footprint of "God particle" found? *The Hindu*. Geneva. Retrieved from http://www.thehindu.com/sci-tech/science/footprint-of-god-particle-found/article3594941.ece

Association for Psychological Science (2010, December 3). Fear of being envied makes people behave well toward others. *Science Daily*. Retrieved December 15, 2013, from http://www.*ScienceDaily*.com /releases/2010/12/101203123601.htm

Association for Psychological Science (2011, December 4). Why do some people never forget a face?. *Science Daily*. Retrieved December 15, 2013, from http://www.*ScienceDaily*.com / releases/2011/12/111202155755.htm

Association for Psychological Science (2011a, January 10). Gesturing while talking helps change your thoughts. *Science Daily*. Retrieved December 15, 2013, from http://www.*ScienceDaily*.com /releases/2011/01/110105121125.htm

Baylor College of Medicine (2011, June 24). Social amoebae rely on genetic 'lock and key' to identify kin. *Science Daily*. Retrieved December 15, 2013, from http://www.*ScienceDaily*.com/releases/2011/06/110623141314.htm

Bellah, R. N. (2011 Oct 5) "Is Humankind's Next Stage of Religious Evolution Here?" Interview with Robert Bella, Templeton Report, http://www.templeton.org/templeton_report/20111005/tr-20111005.pdf

_______ (2011a). *Religion in human evolution : from the Paleolithic to the Axial Age.* Cambridge, Mass.: Belknap Press of Harvard University Press.

Benjamin, A., & McCallum, B. (2008). *A World Without Bees.* London: Guardian Books.

Borenstein, S., & Jordan, R. (2011, February 17). IBM "Watson" Wins: "Jeopardy" Computer Beats Ken Kennings, Brad Rutter. Retrieved December 15, 2013, from http://www.huffingtonpost.com/2011/02/17/ibm-watson-jeopardy-wins_n_824382.html

Brown, N. M. (2010, December 3). The Abacus and The Cross: When the Pope Was A Scientist. *Huffington Post.* Retrieved from http://www.huffingtonpost.com/nancy-marie-brown/when-the-pope-was-a-scien_b_790366.html

Bryner, J. (2012, January 2). Humble People Are More Helpful | Humility & Helpfulness | Pro-Social Behaviors & Positive Psychology | *LiveScience.* Retrieved December 15, 2013, from http://www.livescience.com/17701-humble-people-helpful.html

Bstan-'dzin-rgya-mtsho. (2005). *The Universe in a Single Atom: The Convergence of Science and Spirituality.* New York: Morgan Road Books.

Carnegie Mellon University (2012, February 21). Neuroscientists identify how the brain works to select what we (want to) see. *Science Daily.* Retrieved December 21, 2013, from http://www.*ScienceDaily*.com /releases/2012/02/120221212618.htm

Carter, J., Hudson, C. D., & Reckford, J. T. M. (2012). *NIV lessons from life Bible: Personal Reflections with Jimmy Carter.* Grand Rapids, MI: Zondervan.

Chan, E. (2012). *Harvard Business School Confidential: Secrets of Success*. John Wiley & Sons.

Chang, A. (2011, January 26). Abortion Doesn't Increase Mental Health Risk, But Having A Baby Does. *Huffington Post*. Retrieved December 21, 2013, from http://www.huffingtonpost.com/2011/01/26/abortion-mental-health_n_814582.html

Chang, L. (2006). *Wisdom for the Soul: Five Millennia of Prescriptions for Spiritual Healing*. Gnosophia Publishers.

Chapple, C. K. (1998). Thomas Berry, Buddhism, and the New Cosmology. *Buddhist-Christian Studies*, *18*, 147. doi:10.2307/1390450

Collins, F. S. (2006). *The Language of God : A Scientist Presents Evidence for Belief*. New York ; London: Free.

Dowd, R. M. (2012, April 17). The Evidential Reformation: Humanity Comes of Age. *Huffington Post*. Retrieved from http://www.huffingtonpost.com/rev-michael-dowd/the-evidential-reformation-humanity-comes-of-age_b_1421966.html

Dreher, Rod (2011 July 14), "Quantum Strangeness Goes Macro," *Templeton Report* http://www.templeton.org/templeton_report/20110713/

Elgin, D. (2011, August 27). 4 Misconceptions About the Simple Life. Retrieved December 15, 2013, from http://www.huffingtonpost.com/duane-elgin/four-misconceptions-about_b_937115.html

European Southern Observatory (ESO) (2012, March 28). Many billions of rocky planets in habitable zones around red dwarfs in Milky Way. *Science Daily*. Retrieved December 15, 2013, from http://www.*ScienceDaily*.com/releases/2012/03/120328090937.htm

Feynman, R. P. (1956). The Relation of Science and Religion. Retrieved December 15, 2013, from http://calteches.library.caltech.edu/49/2/Religion.htm

Feynman, R. P., & Leighton, R. (1988). *What Do You Care What Other People Think?: Further Adventures of a Curious Character.* New York: Norton.

Feynman, R. P., Leighton, R. B., & Sands, M. L. (1963). *The Feynman Lectures on Physics.* Reading, Mass.,: Addison-Wesley Pub. Co.

Feynman, R. P., Leighton, Ralph, & Hutchings, E. (1992). *Surely You'reJoking, Mr. Feynman!* London: Vintage.

Geoghegan. (2009, March 3). What's the ideal number of friends? *BBC.* Retrieved from http://news.bbc.co.uk/2/hi/uk_news/magazine/7920434.stm

Gilbert, E. (2010). *Eat, Pray, Love: One Woman's Search for Everything Across Italy, India and Indonesia.* London: Bloomsbury.

Gladwell, M. (2000). *The Tipping Point : How Little Things Can Make a Big Difference* (1st ed.). Boston: Little, Brown.

Goleman, D. (2005). *Emotional Intelligence* (10th anniversary trade pbk. ed.). New York: Bantam Books.

__________ (2006). *Social Intelligence : The New Science of Human Relationships.* New York: Bantam Books.

Graduate Division Berkely. (2011, March 15). Most life on Earth to perish – again? – *Grad News.* Retrieved December 21, 2013, from http://grad.berkeley.edu/news/headlines/sixth-extinction/

Harvard Medical School (2010, December 23). Placebos work -- even without deception. *Science Daily.* Retrieved December 15, 2013, from http://www.*ScienceDaily*.com / releases/2010/12/101222173033.htm

Harvard University (2010, November 17). Language may help create, not just convey, thoughts and feelings. *Science Daily.* Retrieved December 21, 2013, from http://www.*ScienceDaily*.com /releases/2010/11/101103111206.htm

Howard Hughes Medical Institute (2011, March 9). Missing DNA helps make us human. *Science Daily.* Retrieved

December 21, 2013, from http://www.*ScienceDaily*.com / releases/2011/03/110309131934.htm

Huffington, A. (2012, May 15). My Conversation With the Dalai Lama, the": The Convergence of Science and Spirituality, Part 2 (VIDEO). *The Huffington Post.* Retrieved from http:// www.huffingtonpost.com/arianna-huffington/arianna-dalai-lama_b_1519694.html

Iyer, P. (2011, December 29). The Joy of Quiet. *The New York Times.* Retrieved from http://www.nytimes.com/2012/01/01/opinion/ sunday/the-joy-of-quiet.html

_________ (2012). *The Man within My Head* (1st ed.). New York: Alfred A. Knopf.

Johnson, Paul M.& Kenny, Paul J (2010). Dopamine D2 receptors in addiction-like reward dysfunction and compulsive eating in obese rats. *Nature Neuroscience*, 2010; DOI: 10.1038/nn.2519.

Kaleem, J. (2011, September 21). Religion And Science Can Coexist, Scientists Say In New Survey. Retrieved December 15, 2013, from http://www.huffingtonpost.com/2011/09/21/religion-and-science-can-coexist_n_974116.html

Kärkkäinen, V. M. (2004). *Trinity and Religious Pluralism: The Doctrine of the Trinity in Christian Theology of Religions.* Ashgate Publishing, Ltd.

Korzybski, A. (1973). *Science and Sanity: An Introduction to Non-Aristotelian Systems and General Semantics.* Lakeville: Inst. of General Semantics.

Korzybski, A. (n.d.). Map is not the territory. Retrieved December 15, 2013, from http://www.homodiscens.com/home/ways/ loquens/map_territory/index.htm

Krotoski, A. (2010, March 14). Robin Dunbar: We can only ever have 150 friends at most… | Science | The Observer. *The Guardian.* Retrieved December 15, 2013, from http://www.theguardian. com/technology/2010/mar/14/my-bright-idea-robin-dunbar

LaBier, D. (2011, May 17). Why It's So Hard to Find Your Life's Purpose. Retrieved December 15, 2013, from http://www.huffingtonpost.com/douglas-labier/life-purpose_b_862192.html

Loma, T. P., House, B., & Magazine, V. (2012). Marijuana, the Obligatory Pilgrimage, and the Woodstock Generation. Retrieved from http://www.theosophyforward.com/index.php/theosophy/656-marijuana-the-obligatory-pilgrimage-and-the-woodstock-generation.html

Loss of Bees Threatens Global Food System. (2009). *Metaphorical Platypus*. Retrieved December 15, 2013, from http://www.metaphoricalplatypus.com/articles/animals/bees/loss-of-bees-threatens-global-food-system/

Lurie, R. A. (2010, October 17). The Mystical Experience: A Question of What's Beyond. *Huffington Post*. Retrieved from http://www.huffingtonpost.com/rabbi-alan-lurie/the-mystical-experience_b_758082.html

Massachusetts Institute of Technology (2010, December 24). Preplay: How past experiences subconsciously influence behavior. *Science Daily*. Retrieved December 15, 2013, from http://www.*ScienceDaily*.com /releases/2010/12/101222131123.htm

Michaelson, J. (2010, June 11). The Deep Truths are the Simple Ones. Retrieved December 15, 2013, from http://www.huffingtonpost.com/jay-michaelson/spiritual-living-the-deep_b_606330.html

Miller, K. R. (2012, March 1). Science And Religion: Incompatible? *Huffington Post*. Retrieved from http://www.huffingtonpost.com/kenneth-r-miller/post_3059_b_1310826.html

New York University (2012, April 9). Neurological support for Adam Smith's 'theories of morality'. *Science Daily*. Retrieved December 21, 2013, from http://www.*ScienceDaily*.com / releases/2012/04/120409164307.htm

Pandikattu, K. (1996). *Idols Must Die so that Symbols Might Live: Towards an Ontology of Ricœurian Symbols. Faculty of Theology.* Innsbruck, University of Innsbruck. PhD Thesis.

_________ (1999). "Human Freedom: The Finite Quest for the Infinite." *Jnanadeepa: Pune Journal of Religious Studies* 2(2):127-149.

_________ (2000). *Idols to Die, Symbols to Live: Dynamic Interaction Between Language, Reality, and the Divine.* New Delhi, Intercultural Publications.

_________ (2009). "Ever Approachable, Never Attainable: Scientific and Philosophical Reflections on the Human Person." *Omega: Indian Journal of Science and Religion* 8(1): 62-79.

Panikkar, R. (1982). *Blessed Simplicity:The Monk as Universal Archetype.* New York: Seabury Press.

Park, James (2006) *Our Existential Predicament: Loneliness, Depression, Anxiety, & Death* (Minneapolis, MN: Existential Books.

Parkinson's Law. (1955, November 19). *The Economist.* Retrieved from http://www.economist.com/node/14116121

Provine, R. R. (2000). *Laughter : A Scientific Investigation.* New York: Viking.

Pullella, P. (2011, January 6). God was behind Big Bang, universe no accident: Pope | Reuters. Retrieved December 15, 2013, from http://www.reuters.com/article/2011/01/06/us-pope-bigbang-idUSTRE7052OC20110106

Raushenbush, P. B. (2012, March 19). President Jimmy Carter Authors New Bible Book, Answers Hard Biblical Questions. Retrieved December 21, 2013, from http://www.huffingtonpost.com/2012/03/19/president-jimmy-carter-bible-book_n_1349570.html

Robbins, M. (2011, April 14). You Have More Than This Requires. Retrieved December 15, 2013, from http://mike-robbins.com/you-have-more-than-this-requires/

Rossano, M. J. (2010). *Supernatural Selection : How Religion Evolved.* New York ; Oxford: Oxford University Press.

Saey, T. H. (2011, March 9). Missing bits of DNA may define humans. *Science News*. Retrieved December 21, 2013, from https://www.sciencenews.org/article/missing-bits-dna-may-define-humans

Scripps Research Institute (2010, March 29). Compulsive eating shares addictive biochemical mechanism with cocaine, heroin abuse, study shows. *Science Daily*. Retrieved December 21, 2013, from http://www.*ScienceDaily*.com / releases/2010/03/100328170243.htm

Shapiro, E., & Shapiro, D. (2012, May 22). GPS to a Quiet Mind: 6 Meditative Steps to Freedom. Retrieved December 15, 2013, from http://www.huffingtonpost.com/ed-and-deb-shapiro/meditation-tips_b_1531191.html

Sikes, R. S. (2001). Rex Steven Sikes: IDEA Seminars Trainer and Founder. Retrieved December 15, 2013, from http://www.idea-seminars.com/about/rex.htm

Smock, J. (2013, September 26). Lessons From Elizabeth Gilbert (That Don't Involve Eating, Praying, or Loving). *TheHuffington Post*. Retrieved from http://www.huffingtonpost.com/jessica-smock/lessons-from-elizabeth-gi_b_3995263.html

Soares-Prabhu, G., & D'Sa, F. X. (2001). *Theology of Liberation: An Indian Biblical Perspective*. Pune: Distributed by Jnana-Deepa Vidyapeeth.

__________ (2003). *The Dharma of Jesus*. Maryknoll, N.Y.: Orbis Books.

SUNY Downstate Medical Center (2012, April 12). Excessive worrying may have co-evolved with intelligence. *Science Daily*. Retrieved December 21, 2013, from http://www.*ScienceDaily*.com /releases/2012/04/120412153018.htm

Timothy. (2005, April 18). The Early History of Nupedia and Wikipedia: A Memoir - *Slashdot*. Retrieved December 15, 2013, from http://features.slashdot.org/story/05/04/18/164213/the-early-history-of-nupedia-and-wikipedia-a-memoir

Toffler, A. (1970). *Future Shock*. New York,: Random House.

Trinity College Dublin (2012, April 19). How social interaction and teamwork led to human intelligence. *Science Daily*. Retrieved December 21, 2013, from http://www.*ScienceDaily*.com / releases/2012/04/120419132556.htm

Udoewa, V. (2011, September 3). Doubt: A Scientific And Religious Perspective. Retrieved December 15, 2013, from http://www.huffingtonpost.com/victor-udoewa/doubt-as-stepping-stone-t_b_930601.html

University of California - Berkeley (2011, September 23). Scientists use brain imaging to reveal the movies in our mind. *Science Daily*. Retrieved December 15, 2013, from http://www.*ScienceDaily*.com /releases/2011/09/110922121407.htm

University of Chicago (2010, August 17). Marriage and committed romance reduce stress-related hormone production. *Science Daily*. Retrieved December 15, 2013, from http://www.*ScienceDaily*.com /releases/2010/08/100817111827.htm

University of Chicago Medical Center (2011, December 9). Helping your fellow rat: Rodents show empathy-driven behavior, evidence suggests. *Science Daily*. Retrieved December 15, 2013, from http://www.*ScienceDaily*.com /releases/2011/12/111208141933.htm

University of Oregon (2012, February 24). Neither birth nor death stops a flock, new theory shows. *Science Daily*. Retrieved December 21, 2013, from http://www.*ScienceDaily*.com/releases/2012/02/120224111143.htm

University of Oxford (2012, March 24). Brain size may determine whether you are good at keeping friends. *Science Daily*. Retrieved December 15, 2013, from http://www.*ScienceDaily*.com/releases/2012/03/120324145542.htm

University of York (2010, October 5). Neanderthals had feelings too, say researchers. *Science Daily*. Retrieved

December 21, 2013, from http://www.*ScienceDaily*.com/releases/2010/10/101005085505.htm

Vattanky, J. (1984). *Gangesa's Philosophy of God : Analysis, Text, Translation and Interpretation of Isvaravada Section of Gangesa's Tattvacintamani with a Study on the Development of Nyaya Theism*. Madras: Adyar Library and Research Centre.

__________ *A System of Indian Logic : The Nyaya Theory of Inference: Analysis, Text, Translation and Interpretation of the Anumana Section of Karikavali, Muktavali and Dinakari*. Richmond: Curzon.

Vaughan-Lee, L. (2011, May 16). How Our Consciousness Affects the Environment. *The Huffington Post,* Retrieved December 21, 2013, from http://www.huffingtonpost.com/llewellyn-vaughanlee/spirituality-ecology_b_861227.html

Vernon, M. (2005). *The Philosophy of Friendship*. Basingstoke: Palgrave Macmillan.

Wellcome Trust (2011, October 21). Number of Facebook friends linked to size of brain regions, study suggests. *Science Daily*. Retrieved December 15, 2013, from http://www.*ScienceDaily*.com /releases/2011/10/111020025650.htm

Winston, K. (2012, February 22). Grief Without God Is A Challenge For Atheists. *The Huffington Post* Retrieved December 21, 2013, from http://www.huffingtonpost.com/2012/02/21/grief-without-god-challenge-atheists_n_1285359.html

Yale University (2011, March 18). Human prejudice has ancient evolutionary roots. *Science Daily*. Retrieved December 15, 2013, from http://www.*ScienceDaily*.com / releases/2011/03/110317102552.htm

Zbilut, J. P., & Giuliani, A. (2008). *The Latent Order of Complexity*. Nova Publishers.

Index

G

H

I

J

K

L

M

N

O

P